Best Poems of 1973

Best Poems of 1973
Borestone Mountain Poetry Awards 1974

A Compilation of Original Poetry
Published in Magazines of the
English-Speaking World in 1973

Volume 26

Pacific Books, Publishers, Palo Alto, California
1974

Copyright © 1974 by Borestone Mountain Poetry Awards.
All rights reserved.

International Standard Book Number 0-87015-217-3.
Library of Congress Catalog Card Number 49-49262.
Printed and bound in the United States of America.

PACIFIC BOOKS, PUBLISHERS
P.O. Box 558, Palo Alto, California 94302

LIONEL STEVENSON, 1902–1973

Lionel Stevenson was one of the founders of Borestone Mountain Poetry Awards and throughout his busy academic and literary career was a loyal supporter of the project. Upon the death of Robert Thomas Moore in 1958, Dr. Stevenson became chairman of the editorial board, thus resolving the question of whether the project would continue. He remained as chairman until his death in December 1973, when he was working on the present volume, twenty-sixth in the series.

Darwin Among the Poets (University of Chicago Press, 1932) was his first book in the field of poetry. At that time he was head of the English department at Arizona State College. In 1937, he moved to the University of Southern California, where he served as chairman of the English department for eleven years. In 1955, he was appointed the James B. Duke Professor of English at Duke University. Later he served as chairman of the Department of English. After his retirement from Duke University, he was visiting professor at the University of Houston and the University of British Columbia. During his academic career he was visiting professor at seven universities and held a lectureship at the University of Oxford.

Dr. Stevenson was recognized as an authority in both Canadian and Victorian literature. His first published book was *Appraisals of Canadian Literature* (Macmillan, 1926). His collection of Canadian books, started some fifty-five years ago and consisting of more than 500 titles, was given to the Perkins Library at Duke University, where he is now being honored with a showing of his own books and items from the Stevenson Collection of Canadiana. The Duke University Press will publish this year, *Nineteenth-Century Literary Perspectives: Essays in Honor of Lionel Stevenson*, with contributions by leading scholars of the period. He will be remembered for *The Showman of Vanity Fair: The Life of W. M. Thackeray* (Scribner's, 1947), *The Ordeal of George Meredith: A Biography* (Scribner's, 1953) and *The English Novel: A Panorama* (Houghton Mifflin Co., 1960) in mentioning several of the eleven books and more than fifty articles he wrote. He was awarded the 1973 Cup of the Mayflower

Society for his last book, *The Pre-Raphaelite Poets,* published by the University of North Carolina Press in 1972. He is mourned by our staff and the many friends of the Borestone series who believe in the project he so faithfully supported, that of preserving in book form an annual selection of poems that otherwise might be forgotten in the countless pages of magazines.

WADDELL AUSTIN

FOREWORD

Best Poems of 1973 presents the Borestone Mountain Poetry Awards twenty-sixth annual selections from magazines of the English-speaking world issued in 1973. The selections are based upon the few requirements established for the first volume which have remained unchanged throughout the series. A poem is eligible if it is the first printing and not more than one hundred lines. Reprints, translations, and unpublished poems are not considered. The magazines and the issues from which the selections were taken are listed in the "Contents." Poems in the late winter issues that are not available for reading before the close of the selections will be considered for next year's selections.

The editorial procedure has also been consistent throughout the twenty-six volumes. The poems in approximately one hundred and fifty magazines are read by the reading staff, and from these some three hundred poems are selected each year. When the year's selections are complete, copies of the poems are sent to the judges with the names of the authors and magazines deleted, as there is no intention of recognizing established names in preference to newcomers, or apportioning selections between magazines and countries. The judges score their individual preferences and forward the results to the office of the Managing Editor, where a tabulation of the scores determines the final selections. The three highest scores are the winners of the year's cash awards. Thus, there can be more than one poem by the same poet and a number of poems from the same periodical.

"The Birthday" by Philip Dacey received the first award of $300. "Summoned" by Diana O Hehir won the second award of $200, and "Eating Pears at Midnight" by Catharine Savage Brosman received the third award of $100.

The editors gratefully acknowledge permission to reprint these selected poems from the magazines, publishers, and authors owning the copyrights. At the time the selections were completed in March 1974, some poems were scheduled for reprinting in collections of the poets. These subsequent printings and other recognitions are recorded under "Acknowledgments and Notes."

The Editors

LIONEL STEVENSON
  Chairman
HOWARD SERGEANT
  *British Commonwealth
  Magazines
  (except Canada)*

HILDEGARDE FLANNER
FRANCES MINTURN HOWARD
GEMMA D'AURIA
WADDELL AUSTIN
  Managing Editor

ACKNOWLEDGMENTS AND NOTES

"Feeding Time" by Janet Beeler is included in her collection of poems, *How to Walk on Water,* published in 1973 by The Cleveland State University, Poetry Center, Cleveland, Ohio, copyright © 1973 Janet Beeler.

"The Burning" by T. Alan Broughton is reprinted with permission from the February issue of *Yankee Magazine,* published by Yankee, Inc., Dublin, N.H., copyright 1973.

"Huddersfield" by Cal Clothier will appear this spring in *The First International Poetry Society Anthology,* published by HUB Publications, Youlgrave, Bakewell, Derbyshire, England.

Permission to reprint "Hay Fever" is by the author, A. D. Hope, who holds the copyright, and Curtis Brown (Australia) Pty., Ltd.

"Young Delinquent" by John Mays is from *Phoenix,* a poetry magazine published at 8 Cavendish Road, Heaton Mersey, Stockport, Cheshire, England.

"The Heart" by W. S. Merwin is reprinted by permission from *The Hudson Review,* Vol. XXVI, No. 1 (Spring, 1973) and copyrighted © 1973 by *The Hudson Review.*

"To Isabel Who Hid in My Closet in Buenos Aires on Christmas Day, on Christmas Day" by Gary Miranda is reprinted with permission from the December 1973 issue of *Yankee Magazine,* published by Yankee, Inc., Dublin, N.H., copyright © 1973 by Yankee.

"Seals at High Island" by Richard Murphy is reprinted with permission from *The New York Review of Books,* copyright © 1973 Nyrev, Inc. The poem was subsequently reprinted in the April/May issue of *The London Magazine.*

"The Flying Mural" by Les A. Murray will be included in his collection of poems, *Lunch and Counter,* scheduled for publication in August by Angus and Robertson Ltd., Sydney, Australia.

"A New Leaf" by Philip Oakes was subsequently included in his new collection of poems, *Married/Singular,* published in 1974 by Andre Deutsch, Ltd., London.

"Motion and Rest" by Richard Pevear is the new title of the poem "The Killing of Orpheus" and is reprinted by permission from *The Hudson Review,* Vol. XXV, No. 4 (Winter, 1972/73), copyright © by *The Hudson Review.*

"High Frequency" is also from the book *To Be of Use,* copyright 1969, 1971, 1973 by Marge Piercy, and is reprinted by permission of Doubleday & Company, Inc.

"Winter '72" is reprinted by permission of the author, Al Pittman, Memorial University, St. John's, Newfoundland.

"Crystal" and "The Breathers" will be included in James Reiss' collection of poems, *The Breathers,* to be published in September by The Ecco Press, New York.

"From a Survivor" has subsequently been included in *Diving into the Wreck, Poems, 1971-1972* by Adrienne Rich and is reprinted by permission of W. W. Norton & Company, copyright © 1973 by W. W. Norton & Company, Inc.

"Sheep" by Leroy Searle first appeared in *Poetry,* copyrighted © 1973 by The Modern Poetry Association, and is reprinted by permission of the Editor of *Poetry.*

"Ararat" by Jane Shore first appeared in *Poetry,* copyrighted © 1973 by The Modern Poetry Association, and is reprinted by permission of the Editor of *Poetry.*

"Now the Slow Creation" by Kathleen Spivack, copyright © 1973 by The Minneapolis Star and Tribune Company, Inc. from the book *Flying Inland* by Kathleen Spivack, is reprinted by permission of Doubleday & Company, Inc.

"Snake Hunt" and "Slow Country" by David Wagoner subsequently have been included in his new collection of poems, *Sleeping in the Woods,* copyright © 1973 by Indiana University Press and reprinted by permission of the publisher.

"The Country of Everyday: the Dancer" and "The Country of Everyday: the Good Citizen" by Tom Wayman were included in his new book, *For and Against the Moon: Blues, Yells and Chuckles,* published by Macmillan Company of Canada in May of this year, and are reprinted by permission of the publisher.

"Let it Blow" by Reed Whittemore is to be included in a collection of his poems, *The Mother's Breast and the Father's House,* to be published in September 1974 by Houghton Mifflin Company.

The poems "Snake Hunt" (page 125), "After the Creation" (page 137), "Sonora for Sale" (page 105), "John Chapman" (page 136), "Let It Blow" (page 133), "Breasts" (page 25), "Night Patrol" (page 38), "Crystal" (page 89), "A Storm in April" (page 135) and

"Mr. D." (page 110) are copyrighted © 1973 by The New Yorker Magazine, Inc.

We note the following information we have received on copyrights: "The Jesus Infection" and "The Order" copyright © 1973 *The Atlantic Monthly*; "After Song" copyright © 1973 *Commonweal*; "Will There Be Any Stars in My Crown" copyright © 1973 Dabney Stuart.

CONTENTS

Philip Dacey: (*First Award*)	The Birthday	1
	Southern Poetry Review—Vol. XIII, No. 3—Fall	
Diana O Hehir: (*Second Award*)	Summoned	3
	Poetry Northwest—Autumn	
Catharine Savage Brosman: (*Third Award*)	Eating Pears at Midnight	5
	The Georgia Review—Summer	
Janet Beeler:	Feeding Time	6
	Antaeus—Summer	
T. Alan Broughton:	The Burning	8
	Yankee—February	
Jean Burden:	Between These Weathers	9
	Chicago Tribune Magazine—May 20	
Cal Clothier:	Huddersfield	10
	Outposts (England)—No. 98—Autumn	
Steven R. Cope:	Old Wolf	12
	Twigs—X/1	
Margaret Diesendorf:	Light	14
	Poetry Australia (Australia)—No. 46	
John Drew:	Ghosts	15
	Canadian Forum (Canada) March	
Maureen Duffy:	Ode on Rereading Keats	16
	Wave (England)—No. 6—Spring	
Prewitt Edelman:	Caetano	19
	Southwest Review—Spring	
Jessie T. Ellison:	Thoughts on an Unattended Funeral M.M.	21
	Epos—Vol. 24, No. 3—Spring	
Sister Mary Jeremy Finnegan:	After-Song	22
	Commonweal—October 19	
Siv Cedering Fox:	She Used to Water the Plants	23
	The Minnesota Review—Spring	
Tess Gallagher:	Breasts	25
	The New Yorker—March 3	
Kinereth Gensler:	English Is a Foreign Language	27
	Poetry Northwest—Autumn	
Debora Greger:	The Bone's Prayer	28
	Antaeus—Summer	

A. L. Hendriks:	The Construction of Cities	29
	Outposts (England)—Spring	
Kathleen Herbert:	Eve Remembers	30
	English (England)—Summer	
Jean Hollander:	Finally the Manger	32
	Arizona Quarterly—Winter	
John Holloway:	Stony	33
	Outposts (England)—Spring	
A. D. Hope:	Hay Fever	34
	Quadrant (Australia)—April	
Anne Hussey:	The Chandelier	36
	The Beloit Poetry Journal—Winter 72/73	
Josephine Jacobsen:	Night Patrol	38
	The New Yorker—January 6	
Stephen Kennedy:	The Suicide and Sainting of Anselm	39
	Prairie Schooner—Spring	
Krandall Kraus:	The Meeting	41
	Southern Poetry Review—Fall	
Maxine Kumin:	The Jesus Infection	43
	The Atlantic Monthly—October	
Greg Kuzma:	For My Mother and Father Living Apart	45
	Prairie Schooner—Winter	
Greg Kuzma:	The Future	47
	Prairie Schooner—Winter	
Douglas LePan:	Crack-up	48
	Canadian Forum (Canada)—February	
Noel Macainsh:	Metagymnastics	51
	Westerly (Australia)—April	
John Mays:	Young Delinquent	54
	Phoenix (England)—No. 10—July	
W. S. Merwin:	The Heart	56
	The Hudson Review—Vol. XXVI, No. 1—Spring	
Vassar Miller:	Wedding March Off-Key	58
	Southwest Review—Summer	
Gary Miranda:	The Moth-Hand	59
	Poetry Northwest—Autumn	
Gary Miranda:	To Isabel Who Hid in My Closet in Buenos Aires on Christmas Day, on Christmas Day	60
	Yankee—December	

Glenn Morazzini:	The Thirteenth Year	61
	Poet Lore—Vol. 68, No. 4—Winter	
Herbert Morris:	Wallace Stevens' Letters	64
	Salmagundi—Fall	
Richard Murphy:	Seals at High Island	66
	The New York Review of Books—February 22	
Les A. Murray:	The Flying Mural	68
	Poetry Australia (Australia)—No. 46	
Michael Niflis:	Plants	70
	The Virginia Quarterly Review—Summer	
Philip Oakes:	A New Leaf	72
	London Magazine (England)—October/November	
Joyce Carol Oates:	Seizure	74
	The Ohio Review—Fall	
Carole Oles:	Hysterectomy in Munich	76
	Prairie Schooner—Fall	
Mary Oliver:	The Family	78
	Harper's Magazine—February	
Robert Pack:	Pruning Fruit Trees	79
	Prairie Schooner—Fall	
Richard Pevear:	Motion and Rest	81
	The Hudson Review—Vol. XXV, No. 4—Winter 72/73	
Marge Piercy:	High Frequency	83
	Chelsea—No. 35—August	
Al Pittman:	Winter '72	85
	The Fiddlehead (Canada)—Spring	
Neil Powell:	Identities	87
	Workshop New Poetry (England)—No. 21	
James Reiss:	Crystal	89
	The New Yorker—May 12	
James Reiss:	The Breathers	90
	Southwest Review—Summer	
Adrienne Rich:	From a Survivor	92
	Antaeus—Spring	
Vernon Scannell:	Marriage Counsel	93
	New Statesman (England)—July 20	
Vernon Scannell:	Where Shall We Go?	95
	The Times Literary Supplement (England)—December	

Jessie Schell:	Carnival Games	96
	Southern Poetry Review—Spring	
Donald Schenker:	Agoraphobia	98
	Wormwood Review—August 12	
Michael Schmidt:	The Shells	100
	The Critical Quarterly (England)—Winter 72/73	
Leroy Searle:	Sheep	102
	Poetry—February	
Richard Shelton:	Another Darkness	104
	The Ohio Review—Winter	
Richard Shelton:	Sonora for Sale	105
	The New Yorker—December 10	
Jane Shore:	Ararat	106
	Poetry—January	
Robert L. Smith:	Journeys and Changes	107
	The Little Magazine—Winter/Spring	
Kathleen Spivack:	Now the Slow Creation	109
	Harper's Magazine—May	
Ann Stanford:	Mr. D.	110
	The New Yorker—July 9	
Peter Stevens:	The Idea of Water	111
	Quarry (Canada)—Winter	
Joan Stone:	Birthday Poem	113
	The Georgia Review—Winter	
Norma McLain Stoop:	The Order	115
	The Atlantic Monthly—August	
Dabney Stuart:	Will There Be Any Stars in My Crown	117
	The Ohio Review—Spring	
Andrew Taylor:	Beyond Silence II	118
	New Poetry (Australia)—June	
Arthur Vogelsang:	Deer Herd Brings Pumas to Kansas	121
	Northwest Review—Vol. XIII, No. 2	
David Wagoner:	Slow Country	123
	The Southern Review—Winter	
David Wagoner:	Snake Hunt	125
	The New Yorker—April 14	
James E. Warren, Jr.	Lest You, Lest Poetry	126
	The Lyric—Winter	

Tom Wayman:	The Country of Everyday: the Dancer *Canadian Forum* (Canada)—April	127
Tom Wayman:	The Country of Everyday: the Good Citizen *Canadian Forum* (Canada)—April	129
Nancy G. Westerfield:	Footway Crossing a Suspension Bridge, on the Ohio *Twigs*—IX/2	131
Reed Whittemore:	Let It Blow *The New Yorker*—November 5	133
Richard Wilbur:	A Storm in April *The New Yorker*—April 7	135
Richard Wilbur:	John Chapman *The New Yorker*—July 30	136
Paul Zweig:	After the Creation *The New Yorker*—April 21	137

Best Poems of 1973

THE BIRTHDAY

Thirty candles and one
to grow on. My husband
and son watch me
think of wishes.

I wish I found it
easier to make wishes
than I do. Wasn't it,
years ago, easy to make wishes?

My husband and son *are* wishes.
It is as if
every day I wait for them
to happen again,

and they do.
But surely there is much
I am without, yet
I stand here, wishless.

Perhaps I want
what I needn't wish for,
my life: it is
coming, everything will happen.

Or perhaps I want
precisely what I don't know,
all that darkness
so tall and handsome before me.

I have seen women age
beautifully, with a
growing, luminous
sexuality:

now I know, each year
they've been slowly
stepping out of their wishes
like their clothes.

I stand here amazed
at what is happening to me,
how I've begun to lighten
of desires, getting down

to my secret skin,
the impossibly thin
membrane this side
of nothing. Husband,

I wish I could tell you.

       PHILIP DACEY

SUMMONED

Summoned by the frantic powers
Of total recall, sleeping pills, love;
Come down, come down, come down;
Wear red if you can, wear red
For suffering, jade for rebirth,
Diamonds in your front incisors,
A rope of orange stars—you were martyred, weren't you?
So wear a circle of gold thorns, prongs capped
In scarlet shell.

And bring with you, down, down, down,
A recollection of how you fell
Like Lucifer, morn to morn and night to night
For at least a year, your hair alight
Your rigid corpse a spoked wheel
Meteor trails ejecting from each thumb,
Sun eyes, a black light in your chest
Where the bare heart burned.

Oh, love, my love, my failure,
I can hardly bear, barely recall
The nights I ate ghosts, the nights
My shuttered, shivered window held
Three million savage stars and you;
Your spread arms splitting my sky, the light
Reflected in my own eye: your light, your might, your burn.

Come down. My sky-chart shows
Your cold corpse turning slowly, a black sun
Giving no light at all, reflecting none,
Aimlessly gentle, like a twig on a pond
Circling. Gone, they say, gone, truly gone.
The eyes as blank as buttons, the mouth
Only an O. Never mind. Come down.

I can revive you. My passion is Judah, all artifice, all God.
I care with my breasts. I care with my belly's blood.
Come down.

                                          Diana O Hehir

EATING PEARS AT MIDNIGHT

The others are mostly asleep, the child
wrapped close to her original peace; alone
in the kitchen, I treat myself to gourmandise,
seasoned with an old feel of nostalgia.

All the windows open onto an October night,
mild, where a pale light dips in pools left
from the evening rain, and the honeysuckles
still bloom over the fence. How sweet

the air, and then the juicy autumn pear,
purloined from myself and tomorrow's salad,
enjoyed in stealth as a silent companion—
making insomnia delicious. On the porch,

the dog, half-blind, whines from old age,
his seventeen years weightier than my own
thirty-seven. Thinking forth, I cannot guess
what I shall know on that same edge of ruin,

later—but could wish it like this night,
a solitude to be made use of, a wakefulness
that calls the senses out from their dull
custom, to taste a full, ripe fruit;

then memory will feast, with the rosy
peeling falling around, bruises cut out,
one's dark self as company, and time
like a telescope pulling down the stars.

        CATHARINE SAVAGE BROSMAN

FEEDING TIME

Dusk again at the Old Forge dump.
Black heads honed with hunger
peer through the closing green,
then the bears emerge
furred in pitch shadows.

In this green light they seem to float
graceful as whales,
paddling at boxes of fish heads,
diving under crates of cabbage leaves,
their kitchen submerged in mist
and sinking deeper into the night stream.

My flashlight fixes two cubs in a fresh pit,
sucking on cider jugs
until their mother knocks them tumbling
to a treasure of beef bones
already sticking white as fingers
pointing from her teeth.

Grey muzzle, scarred hide,
fruit peel silver in his mouth,
only the oldest bear regards me.
He is the one I come to see,
and he drifts closer every night,
stiff-jointed,
his fur shined with slobber.
His flat black eyes
cleave to me as he eats.
After all these nights of watching
I have a place now in his hunger.

But what place has he in mine,
this great grey bear
stinking of fish and mud,

this enormous longing
feeding on my dreams each night?

    JANET BEELER

THE BURNING

He died in the woodpile
curled in clenched intensity
of spite, stinger out
and honey-striped body
stroked to the wood
to make the axe's wound seem flesh.
I had uncovered summer's heat;
the wood released
a bitter, green-sap smell,
the bee seemed heavily poised
with juice, dazed
and lost from the comb.
But nights of frost
had slowed him down,
and choosing not to sleep away
he thrust and died.

I carried that log
like a litter in the dark
and set it in the hearth
to watch flames rise and take
the body on its bark.
Caught in the heat, the wings
were beating and gathering fire
to fill the night they entered humming,
taking the dark for a comb.
Now the fling of wintered air
between my bare boards and the roof
stings me and I yearn to rise
away from honeyed forms,
to turn in anger from embraces
and find at last
the fiery touch of consummation.

T. Alan Broughton

BETWEEN THESE WEATHERS

Neither bound
nor set free,
I wobble on your wrist
like some crazy, drunken thing,
not knowing up from down,
nor friend from prey.

Why am I here, I say?
I, more wing
than claw,
peck at this tether,
yet hunger for your hand
both flesh and metaphor.

The sun says wait,
the night says fly.
Between these weathers and these hopes
I hesitate.
The earth turns green and golden.
The dark sky
opens like a door.

     JEAN BURDEN

HUDDERSFIELD

for Michael Kruszynski, Composer

Huddersfield survives for me
not on a map of coloured inks
but in the scribbled nerveways of my brain,
as indestructible as Pennine water
or the wintered silhouette of Scapegoat Hill.

There is the town of stone,
of wool and history, that solid place where I once lived;
and then there is the town which lives in me
and like the town which lived my childhood out
it lines my veins and rings my trunk, and has a root
deep in the way I move towards tomorrow.

This town survives
among the terraced sootfalls of my mind
where darkening time
itself grows old, and I grow old, but will not die
until my cells of thoughtful blood
forget themselves again in earth.
Were Huddersfield cut out of me
I would remain a leaf in partial skeleton.

Going about the town of stone today
I recognise it as a tune I know
played out of key, or my own voice played back on tape.
Old buildings have been scoured to new;
new buildings look as cardboard drab
as packing cases in a station yard.

So I must confess I miss
the Market Hall, that old iron reptile house
which stank of bacon, soap and sweaty socks;
and the station, black as old Victoria,
in Saint George's Square, its pigeoned columns
conducting us to hell in classic style.

Many parts of town are little changed
or changed no more nor less than I have changed
since I last walked in them. Haunting myself
in New North Road, I know the pavement yard by yard
in my imagination, watch myself stepping up and
down the kerbs at every minor road and drive.
I sense the temperature of my shoes, my shadow's density,
the active weight of stepping up and down.
Yet if I went there now to walk
with maps supplied from memory, I would soon fall.

And if along that well-known unknown road
I were to meet myself as I was then, so newly
educated but so lightly skilled in living,
like strangers, he and I soon discover
silence books and talk could never span.

What I am now, but he could not yet comprehend,
is everything I learned from those I knew
and those I loved — and loving leapt from child
to fatherhood: it is the darker foliage
my sapling years began to make and that deep root
to knowledge of myself amid the world, which took to life
nourished in the stones of Huddersfield.

CAL CLOTHIER

OLD WOLF

Although wolves don't often come
To howl outside my window,
Last night one did. Just one,
While the others sat back
On haunches and watched his moves,
His circlings, his years of experience.

A circle, trampled to the earth by
His restless feet, seemed a deep well
From my upstairs window; and he,
Unable to climb the snowy wet
Walls of his prison and, being old,
Too conditioned to admit defeat,

Paced and sat, always within the circle,
And raised his nose in the
Exact same spot, and howled at the
Same moon above his head and mine

Until I slipped quietly down the stairs
To peep around the curtain, in full
View of the truth. Then he was a wolf.
Old wolves have faces marred by
Unrest and bad consciences. But, after all,
It's their life to kill, and

Mine to stay alive.

So I shot him, in full view of
His starving family. And they watched
Him growl and not back down,
And felt him knowing
That an old wolf must provide

For his family, one way or another, himself or the man.
But I made him look like a failure.

>   STEVEN R. COPE

LIGHT

for E.P.

There is much about light that we don't understand:
the way it gathers in a man
                        suddenly
to shine with the brightness of ten thousand watts
from his eyes
              I have seen
lakes form on my mother's hand
                              when she cut
the bread in the halo of the wartime
                                    carbide lamp
(the bread shared out to us)
                        in those lakes
my childish soul would drown
                            with the dread
of her loss
          or ride upstream the sinuous
blue rivers of the veins to land
                              in the precincts of her heart
(the chart is now familiar on the back
of my own hand)
                  I have known light to weave brilliant scarves
that dazzled and choked and I cried
                              for the bitter consoling dark
and again
          who can explain
the radiance of my small dead brother
                                laid out in the white carton
coffin fresh in my stiffly
                    starched muslin
with the pink rose pattern
                        (my best-loved) —
his sweet face smooth as porcelain
                          and luminous
AH LUMINOUS

MARGARET DIESENDORF

GHOSTS

Ghosts? Yes, the house has more than its share of ghosts,
Some clearly exposed in old photographs.
But the men who move in the bric à brac of broken pipes
And pens aren't poltergeists. The man who laughs

In painting the scowl on the face of the artisan
On the wall — a new safety match
Damned lucifer, won't light on the bowl of his pipe —
Is Samuel James. His watercolour lets us snatch

A glimpse of the man he is, my father's grandfather.
Upstairs the working man, seemingly quiet-spoken
Formally dressed in the photograph, was first socialist
On the County Council. Now they'd call him token

If they didn't, as they don't, read the reports of uproar
My mother keeps in the cupboard — this is her father.
The crested swagger stick in the hall belongs to Sam
Some sort of collateral uncle, said to have been rather

Sweet on the ladies, thought to have been in the Buffs
As an R.S.M. but since he used to acquire
Chicken wire overnight for the hens he may have come
By the swagger stick in the way he came by the wire.

The erratic clock on my father's desk stands where it stopped
The day my father died. While on the high shelf
Letters home from a boy I have heard them talk about
More remote than an ancestor — are from myself.

Ghosts, all these rumours and myths. Ghosts even the swallows
Nesting under the eaves. Ghosts, the voices below.
For the biggest ghost of them all is the house
I left three thousand miles away twenty years ago.

JOHN DREW

ODE ON REREADING KEATS

No sir I will not; see I
dignify or abuse you with my own age
as if the month we shared
fell too in the same year
calling you, bright boy, sir.
You come to me, darkling
masked in my childhood
with the long dried elder flowers of wreaths
verse epitaphs through these pent streets
and tell me follow into that country
of eglantine and blackthorn
but it is winter and in any case
all my musk roses are dedicate
you come a life too late.

Then I might have followed you
wanting fame too and half in love
with your prints, my steps
tracked so precisely, nine and fourteen
as if we shared the same sock size
I might step into your shoes.
Easeful I leant upon my window sill
into the fading day and saw you
dopple ganging through the fields
under a green sky warping to purple
and thought I might run out
to become you going down with the sun
ghosts walk at twilight
with kindlier beckon than at night.

Now you start at me out of
the pages trailing my life and yours like cerecloth
gibe that my day with its sweets
is gone too, that my years betray

our common growing pain.
It's easy to die, remember.
If she would with her own soft hands
pour me oblivion I could
slip out with a kiss as if
I was just going to move Venus' car
but I hover on her threshold
on the end of my hope
that she will unleash my bounding
and whistle me into the sun.

Too late you come over the black fields
set in winter. I have forgot
betrayed nothing you taught me
about beauty and truth only that
at last wandering my years
like countries I have resolved
that examination question you put
to the ages: she being all truth
is beauty, being beauty is
all my truth. At night she
holds me by permission
of that fancy elf. Apart I
wade through blood, give goblins
guest room, ride nightmare widdershins.

I sip my vintage, seven year they say
matured still not as old as me.
Painstakingly I pass the milestone ages
when it's significant to die: young at thirty-five
choosy at forty or straddling the century's turn
inelegant posture with the legs apart
and easily brought down, til I don't care.
If I had known her then when we walked
rehearsing our verses in beechen green
drawing our rebel bows at wands
I might have gone glad to an early grave.
Now let me limp on as long as we can

armour ourselves with love against swords
she quicken into fancy with my words.

MAUREEN DUFFY

CAETANO

MANUEL	I admire your death, Caetano.
CAETANO	
ALCHEMIST	In muted city street
GOLDSMITH	common and drab as a sparrow's back
MAGICIAN	where pewter and umber sleep
HANGED IN	you mastered at last
A GOLDEN	sheer brilliance of song
CLOAK	without singing
ON A	keen song and ordered
GILDED	by the wind-crafted light
GALLOWS	dazzling around your tomb.
BERLIN	
1709	Those who believed, Caetano,
DECREED	heard you heavy on the golden tree
BY THE	and thought it a flight of eagles
KING OF	on fire and free
PRUSSIA	their wings spilling mortality
AS A	like music in the Prussian night.
WARNING	Nor could they tell
TO	ascent from fall
IMPOSTERS	until they brought you down.

PREWITT EDELMAN

THOUGHTS OF AN UNATTENDED FUNERAL M.M.

I imagine you
in a decorated box
having delicately elaborate silver handles
perhaps a candle or two;
your little bones arranged
with utmost dignity
in death, as in life,
and a deserted music, unchallenged
and unchanged
by your new silence.

I imagine you
carried away swiftly
in the claws of a great golden eagle
to the exploding heart of the sun,
a small, cool darkness
carefully contained
in its own discipline for survival
within the fires.

I imagine you
deep in the belly of the great whale of death,
sounding
to the bottom of the world,
a tiny, fierce point of light
inextinguishable
within vast darknesses.

I imagine you
riding the shining disk
of a giant pendulum
to the exact locality of its rest,
dead center,
the precise moment of arrival
being the precise moment of departure,

which you understood,
Marianne.

I imagine you at last
a seed in the gold and scarlet heart
of a pomegranate,
needing no further
protection.

        JESSIE T. ELLISON

AFTER-SONG

'I lean'd my back unto an aik
I thocht it was a trustie tree;
But first it bow'd and syne it brak . . .'

O rooted in fidelity
and tallest in hieratic cloak—
We thought it was a trusty tree.

Incense abased to vapid smoke,
the aura of Melchisidek
diminishing to legendry.

In coldness borne across the sea
what unpropitious voices spoke
that first it bowed and then it broke?

On earth reverberant with shock
the sacred balm flows waywardly.

We thought it was a trusty tree.

    Sister Mary Jeremy Finnegan

SHE USED TO WATER THE PLANTS

twice a week
then
every morning
then she started to transplant
take cuttings
fertilize

she moved the plants out doors
in the spring: more room
more light
she planted seeds, grafted trees
sprayed roses and pruned

she said the names of the flowers
softly as if they were children
she rehearsed the latin
forming the words with care
a stilted music, lovely and

foreign. "a flower bed
is as good a bed as any"
she said
when her husband left her
there was no question
of loss

he returned once
carried her in from the garden
washed the soil off her feet
and cleaned the dirt from under her nails
with a paring knife

in the morning
the bed was full of crushed leaves

petals
and small clouds
of yellow
pollen

SIV CEDERING FOX

BREASTS

The day you came
this world got its hold on me.
Summer grass and the four of us pounding hell
out of each other for God knows what
green murder of the skull.
Swart nubbins, I noticed you then,
my mother shaking a gritty rag from the porch
to get my shirt on this minute. Brothers,
that was the parting of our ways, for then
you got me down by something else than flesh.
By the loose skin of a cotton shirt
you kept me to the ground
until the bloody gout hung in my face like a web.

Little mothers, I can't find your children.
I have looked in a man
who moved through air like a god.
He brought me clouds
and the loose stars of his goings.
Another kissed me on a pier in Georgia,
but there was blood on his hands,
bad whiskey in the wind. The last one,
he made me a liar until I stole
what I could not win. Loves,
what is this mirror you have left me in?

I could have told you at the start
there would be trouble
from other hands, how the sharp mouths
would find you where you slept.
But I have hurt you as certainly
with cold sorrowings as anyone,
have come the long way
over broken ground to this softness.
Good clowns, how could I know all along

it was your blundering mercies kept me alive
when heaven was a luckless dream?

TESS GALLAGHER

ENGLISH IS A FOREIGN LANGUAGE

English is a foreign language I was born speaking,
a place I live in, like my house

and, like it, foreign to my waking feet
that slide to the edge of morning without knowing

what floor they'll touch—which house,
what hemisphere. Or if the floor will tilt

and they again will find themselves on deck,
waiting for winches to lower the lifeboat.

The one sure speech I know is born of water.
It comes in answer to foghorns, sirens, bells—

vibrations that a foot responds to.
It is the sound of total breath released

when, poised above stopped engines, one first hears
the pumps take hold.

I wake each morning as I woke then,
speaking the language of the new undrowned.

Kinereth Gensler

THE BONE'S PRAYER

That I may keep myself hollow,
an instrument of the wind.
That I may keep the darkness within me
while outside I am light.
That in my place under the surface
I move with animals' grace.
That I may share the silence
of a family of bones.
That I may be the cage of the dreamer's sleep,
if not of his spirit.
That I may be the final home of the lost.
That broken I fulfill the wish.

DEBORA GREGER

THE CONSTRUCTION OF CITIES

Is it an old lure, the construction of cities?
A wayfarer's dream, a mirage of comforts
Blossoming out of wasteplaces and deserts
To cosset and assuage the heart's cold stone
When it is dry, dry as the mind's thin ashen bone?
Is it an old thirst no one cares about or pities?

Were there once silken girls, girls who fed
Desolate voyagers with wine and sweetmeats?
The ones who moved sinuously upon clean sheets
Naked with silver limbs, and others bringing
Fruit and scented garments, still others singing?
Or is it an old fancy hugged in a madman's head?

Were there once kings? Kings powered on their thrones?
Judges who judged commoners along with kings as people?
Archbishops whose prayers rose higher than the steeple?
Lawyers whose compassion ranged far beyond the law?
And unarmed people not in dread? All we saw
Were executioners armed with executive telephones.

Was here once a forum? A passionate debate?
And new philosophy constantly from the flower of intellect?
This is what we came for, what we were led to expect
Here, and in theatres, colleges, where the wise foregather.
What we heard were choruses of casuistic blather
Anxiously mixed with a petulant self-hate.

What we found was boredom, middleclass discomforts
Beyond our imagining: a kind of bland despair;
No one who could bother; no one who could care;
Women in whose sour breasts the gift of giving dies
Breeding children incapable of wonder or surprise,
And men's faces, hollow, turned toward wasteplaces and deserts.

                                        A. L. HENDRIKS

EVE REMEMBERS

In the spring the fabulous tree put out small blossom,
Covered itself all over with white flowers flushing
Pink at the centre, exuded a perfume pregnant
With curious promise. All the plants in the garden
Were excessively scented; this one was different,
Or it seemed so. You must remember it was forbidden.
Alone in that lavish display the tree was unlawful.
There was a paradox in this waxen florescence,
An innocence that was evil.
                              I took to watching
The petals fall to the ground and the apples forming
Green on the branches. The garden was uneventful,
Beautiful but unchanging, suspended and timeless,
Held in eternity like a dream of perfection
Utterly static. Frankly I found it unnerving.
Only the tree was shaping itself to the seasons,
Forcing the flower to fall and the fruit to harden,
Using the sun and the rain and the soil of Eden
For its own private advantage.
                               I doubt whether Adam
Gave it a thought or noticed my growing abstraction,
—In any case he would take my obedience for granted—,
Bored, but resigned, one day much like another,
He lorded it over the beasts with his upright stature,
His human discernment. He was, of course, quite splendid.
Was that imperious torso really a rib short?
Was I bonded so closely bone to his bone aching
In separation? Was that the problem? On looking back
I very much doubt it.
                      Nor do I think the prompting
Came from the serpent. There were all manner of creatures
Roaming the garden, all of them gentle and guileless,
The snake especially. It is true that I loved it;
It would slide its length down the trunk from the skied branches
To coil in my arms, pliant and limpidly trusting;

The warmth of its weight on my heart filled me with longing,
The snake and the tree together held my enchantment.
Slowly the summer passed; the apples became transparent,
Speckled and golden.
                    In the cool of the evening
God would walk in the garden communing with Adam.
Naturally I was excluded so priestly a counsel,
But the animals paused, sensing the hush of his passing,
And even the birds stopped singing. Adam was weakened,
Rendered receptive, a soul enraptured with loving.
I loosened my hair, a web where my beauty flickered
Imponderable as a petal—how lightly falling—
Quietly I lifted my arms to the laden branches
Took the forbidden fruit, the core of the world in my hand.

                                    KATHLEEN HERBERT

FINALLY THE MANGER

Friday the dreamt-of manger gathered its moss,
some curious, creeping shepherds, Arabs calling,
a peasant lantern raising, not trusting to the star,
the upward staring cows, one dull sheep grazing,
a woman bringing water, dancing flutes of boys,
and burdened with their gifts and coming, the kings,
small at the edge of joy. Caught in the bending knee,
the marbled eye, two thousand years refract
and petrify to natural the dubious event.
Still Joseph gazes, tangential always in the fated round
of beast and child, and Mary, amazoned,
kneels tranquil in her ring of love and pain
and curves her robe around the concentrated flesh.

JEAN HOLLANDER

STONY

What can we turn but
    stone faces now, showing
we have an abiding
    weather of erosion

of we do not know what
    but that it is this way
men and women nakedly
    have a way of saying

how turn but
    you now this way, me that way,
and so stonily
    make a concession

to we do not know what
    event of weathering
denudes men and women
    to a way of seeing

where turn but
    inward ... to facingness
and reflection ... to this
    recognition?

        JOHN HOLLOWAY

HAY FEVER

Time, with his scythe honed fine,
Takes a pace forward, swings from the hips; the flesh
Crumples and falls in windrows curving away.
Waiting my turn as he swings — (Not yet, not mine!)
I recall the sound of the scythe on an earlier day:
Late spring in my boyhood; learning to mow with the men;
Eight of us mowing together in echelon line,
Out of the lucerne patch and into the hay,
And I at the end on the left because I was fresh,
Because I was new to the game and young at the skill —
As though I were Time himself, I remember it still.

The mild Tasmanian summer; the men are here
To mow for my minister father and make his hay.
They have brought a scythe for me. I hold it with pride.
The lucerne is up to my knee, the grass to my waist.
I set the blade into the grass as they taught me the way;
The still dewy stalks nod, tremble and tilt aside,
Cornflowers, lucerne and poppies, sugar-grass, summer-grass, laced
With red-stemmed dock; I feel the thin steel crunch
Through hollow-stalk milk thistle, self-sown oats and rye;
I snag on a fat-hen clump; chick-weed falls in a bunch,
But sorrel scatters; dandelion casts up a golden eye,
To a smell of cows chewing their cuds, the sweet hay-breath:
The boy with the scythe never thinks it the smell of death.

The boy with the scythe takes a stride forward, swings
From the hips, keeping place and pace, keeping time
By the sound of the scythes, by the swish and ripple, the sigh
Of the dying grass like an animal breathing, a rhyme
Falling pat on the ear that matches the steel as it sings
True through the tottering stems. Sweat runs into my eye.
How long to a break? How long can I hold out yet?
I nerve my arms to go on; I am running with, flooding with sweat.

How long ago was it? — Why, the scythe is as obsolete now
As arrows and bow. I have lived from one age to another;
And I have made hay while I could and the sun still shone.
Time drives a harvester now: he does not depend on the weather.
Well, I have rolled in his hay, in my day, and now it is gone;
But I still have a barn stacked high with that good dry mow,
Shrivelled and fragrant stems, the grass and the flowers together
And a thistle or two in the pile for the prick of remorse.
It is good for a man when he comes to the end of his course
In the barn of his brain to be able to romp like a boy in the heap....
To lie still in well-cured hay ... to drift into sleep.

A. D. Hope

THE CHANDELIER

We had eyed the empty mansion for weeks
it was locked behind wrought iron gates
like a vicious dog

we worked open a pantry window
in broad daylight the rooms were bare
and we left small sneaker prints
in the dust on the parquet floors
a double staircase met in a center landing
then split again like a fat hourglass
in the ballroom sun from the south windows
recoiled in a billion particles of color
from a crystal chandelier high on the ceiling
we poked at it with a pole
and it started to sway
we poked harder and it swung it swung
back and forth and around its
crystals chiming its crystals
reflecting off the floor and walls

as it grated and ground like an old porch
swing swinging its crazy lights
and clattering music and its music lit
we swayed with it like a cobra
we got drunk on it we
swirled with it it was
a wild ocean our eyes danced
on the surface up and up
on the swell and then
the fixture snapped
it fell
on the upswing it came down
a bomb a geyser shooting frozen
particles into every corner notes
splashed like paints against the walls

we stood the ocean stopped
we had killed it quiet a pile of dead
diamonds a pile of sharp eyes
we moved closer many were
broken some were perfect
greedy collectors novice crooks eight
years old we matched our avarice
with speed we scattered and scrambled
on our knees we crammed
our pockets with all shapes
and cuts we gathered
jewels up in our shirtfronts
and with our bellies showing
we lit out

weeks later we would be
the one-eyed children
in the tree squinting down through
prisms at the houses houses
dizzily trying to touch in the facets single-
handed single-eyed trying to keep our
balance who else but us
could see a green dog go off four
ways at once in a sunburst we swore
on blood we'd never tell and never
get caught with one eye closed
stalking the neighborhood

Anne Hussey

NIGHT PATROL

Washington

The wolf's cousin,
then gentled to clown for us,
paces now, forbidden
to be trusted, or trust—
paces the pavement.

The black shoes and the furry toes
pace together on the wide
street; from the raw light pace
into the shadows' jungle.
The wolf blood courses under hide.
The feet echo; silent go the paws.

A clock strikes winter.
Hunters are cold as hunted.
The dog teaches the man to listen—
something waits in the shadows' center.
The wolf heart knows what is wanted,
called back from a dream unnatural and human.

They walked like mutant friends in a season's sun.
Now they walk like wolves, and know their own.
Their own move toward them; empty, the street
moves toward them where in this bitter season
cold wolf and wolf meet.

JOSEPHINE JACOBSEN

THE SUICIDE AND SAINTING OF ANSELM

    Anselm finds himself ancient in his own right
    like an Ananas pineapple.
                           a wild
    parakeet leaves its bodily rewards
    in his composing room (nobody knows
    Anselm composed) where, bedridden, tired
    angels scrape barnacles off the bottom
    of Anselm's model ships
                           with their wings.

    his eyes write good-byes on his treatises
    which read like maps without legends and lines.
    forced to act as his own godfather at birth
    he continues
               to irrigate his non-
    existent roots. father, siblings, mother,
    all issued out of life, jabbering with fire.

    as a last salve, in his wine-cellar
    he imitates a shrike, and indented
    with work, the shrew-mouse scrabbling in hunger
    over the dirt floor.
                     theology kicks him
    in the stomach, malicious with meaning.

    a lark sits on the sentence of a branch
    outside Anselm's window, making commas
    in the bark, looking for worms to invite
    into its parenthesis of pain.
                         life

starves itself out for Anselm, for some long
inside sense of things: a period. an
angel, bored with its scraping motions,

descends from its bed of ideas,
                                  beats
the dust from its wings, like a gnat, and flies
to the question marks of Anselm's final ribs.

                    STEPHEN KENNEDY

THE MEETING

Instead of giving up an hour
after you are due, I move
to the mirror to inspect my hair,
skirt, contort to view the rear
as you will see it if I leave
the room. I sweep the floor

again. Put off for the moment
reaching to flick
the lamp dead. My undressing
is a study in control, expressing
nothing, as I pick
myself apart in deliberate motions.

Today I plumbed fears of every size—
flowers, confessions, death, a terrible truth—
and was ready, ready for it all,
save your not coming. Tomorrow you'll call
brimming with reasons. Smooth
it over, perhaps apologize.

I will be casual: Nothing to worry about . . .
But already I see you wending with the rest,
eager for comfort, a winsome woman
to change the bed, convert your seed to sanguine
immortality. This is best:
pause, shudder, fade out.

For my part, I preserve the honesty of my single room,
take pleasure from a magazine,
anticipate calls from long distances.
Consider the alternatives: waiting upon fortune,

writing verse, sleeping for dreams.
My life has a good chance.

KRANDALL KRAUS

THE JESUS INFECTION

Jesus is with me
on the Blue Grass Parkway going eastbound.
He is with me
on the Old Harrodsburg Road coming home.
I am listening
to country gospel music
in the borrowed Subaru.
The gas pedal
and the words
leap to the music.
Oh throw out the lifeline!
Someone is drifting away.

Flags fly up in my mind
without my knowing
where they've been lying furled
and I am happy
living in the sunlight
where Jesus is near.
A man is driving his polled Herefords
across the gleanings of a cornfield
while I am bound for the kingdom of the free.
At the little trestle bridge that has no railing
I see that I won't have to cross Jordan alone.

Signposts every mile exhort me
to Get Right With God
and I move over.
There's a neon message blazing
at the crossroad
catty-corner to the Burger Queen:
Ye Come With Me.
Is it well with my soul, Jesus?
It sounds so easy

to be happy after the sunrise,
to be washed in the crimson flood.

Now I am tailgating
and I read the bumper sticker
on a Ford truck full of Poland Chinas.
It says: Honk If You Know Jesus
and I do it.
My sound blats out for miles
behind the pigsqueal
and it's catching in the front end,
in the axle,
in the universal joint,
this rich contagion.

We are going down the valley on a hairpin turn,
the swine and me, we're breakneck in,
we're leaning on
the everlasting arms.

Maxine Kumin

FOR MY MOTHER AND FATHER LIVING APART

I walk a straight road between here and
there, my mother prays I get better, my
father goes on about his chores. Even now
he is standing up the storm windows and
staring deep into them. Even now she is
readying her hands. They love me about
the same. They love me in the dark and
in the day. I love them about the same.
They both want me to continue being good
and getting better. I pray they live
a long time. I pray they survive all
notions they now live by. I pray they
sit down one night and open the pages of
a book and find everything I think I am.
I pray they tell me how to think about
myself when they find out.

And I have always counted on them. Miles
apart from them I see their faces clearly.
Years from their house I return to them
nightly or in poems. I set the boat of the
poem upon the surface of the lake of them.
I go out onto it. I note how it is rough,
how the water is yellow from turning its
bottom up. I note how there is some wind
but there is more than that at work.
Even when calm I look down deep into their
faces and find my own. Even when I am most
looking for them they make me see myself.

And so they have protected me all these
years. And so, broken, separate, in their
single houses, they unite in my mind,
hands locked, coupled in bed, sharing the
driving on the long trip East, passing

the salt. And so they have saved me from
turning sharp corners. And so they have
stayed together for being so long together.
When I go to them I go to both. I know
where to find them. I turn my eyes around.
I make my shoulders small, I throw off what
I have done in my name. I go to the closet,
any closet, and there are my trousers fresh
ironed, there are the shirts my mother
picked out for me. I put on my clothes and
go down to where my father works. I
take hold of the other end of what he
is doing, and hold it.

                                              GREG KUZMA

THE FUTURE

I have gone to one edge where I can look down
and see nothing. The price of admission is
my daughter's high-pitched laughter. Now it is
gone she dedicates herself to service to others,
to the conservation of energy within the body politic.
My knee no longer amuses her.

I have gone to another edge where I look down
and see nothing. The price of admission is how
the bellow goes out of my son's laughter. Now it is
gone from him he stands straight as a ruler, and
jots down things to remember later.

It is almost easy to fall back on loneliness,
to let my hands folded be the temple of my search,
to let the room anoint itself with silence,
the books on the shelves the mouths of dead men
cheer me on.

I imagine a land in which the wind blows no change,
the cliffs are padded, the rivers meet each other
and shake hands. A land where books break down
into tears.

In the land of the future night is falling.
My children raise themselves by sheer acts of the
will, and I am nowhere to be found.

GREG KUZMA

CRACK-UP

Stove in, the flesh he was travelling in, his face
punched full of figures. A fluke from leviathan
caught him and he capsized, down down
in a dry death. Accountants searching
his failure with rubber-gloved hands drew out
a typical balance-sheet of delicate red frustrations,
a whole corporation of losses.

So far nothing so very unusual, nothing
that couldn't be cured by a simple proceeding in bankruptcy,
the creditors paid off at ten cents on the dollar, with nobody
else any the wiser (after all
the streets are full of the dead, the disfigured, and the
   walking wounded).
But this casualty wouldn't behave as though nothing had
   happened,
kept calling for his mother, made water in the streets, and
   cried and cried,
and wouldn't be comforted even when they told him
of all the ten-lane highways they were building for him
and the shopping plazas and the new planetarium.
Clearly that couldn't go on. Not when
raccoons began infesting the city
and a deer blundered one morning into the stock-exchange.
There was even a rumour that a unicorn had been seen in
   the suburbs.

In secret session the city fathers declared him officially dead,
and authorized the coroners to conduct an autopsy,
and investigate, and report, with full powers
under the Public Enquiries Act.
When they picked him up he was standing at a street-corner
singing "Love, I laid my love away" — a song of his own
that sounded a little like "Careless Love," only slower and sadder
as he sung it with tears streaming down

as though he were mourning for a boat stove in and drifting
away, lost love, lost hope, with tissues unravelling into the gutter.
He came quietly, and answered their questions as well as
   he could.
How had it all begun? He couldn't remember exactly,
but he had always been good at games . . . . . What could that
have to do with it? Well, the guidance teacher
suggested he might go on into games theory and linear
   programming,
and before long he was in charge of a whole room of
   key-punch operators.
Soon he moved over to Acetates Unlimited to run
their sampling and forecasting. He had been getting along
   famously, then,
whatever happened? His big break came (this said with a
   sigh, a deep sigh)
when he was appointed to Defence Research as head econometrist.
"You had it made. Come, what was it happened?"
"One morning I was examining one of the models when
a variable shifted and I fell, it must have been thirty feet.
I felt as though I'd broken my back.
Sometimes I think I'd be better off dead."

He didn't whimper when they sliced back his muscles
and cut open his gut and took out the organs.
But when they reached for his sex he screamed like a bird,
his flesh switched to scrap, his nerves wires, his eyes
deflowered through the sockets of his skull
till they flowered again in immaculate spirals of copper foil,
his spine coiled with rust-proof tubing.
And he slid from the mortuary-slab
and strode invulnerably away.

Clanking a little as he went, he moved through
the market with exemplary candour
offering for sale skeins of perfectly machined ball-bearings
and nickel-alloy prospects sprouting from his shoulders.
No takers, though.

But now he has found his niche.
A businessman of imagination has seen his possibilities
and bought him lock stock and barrel
to hang (as a warning? as a guide to the future?)
over the door of the aluminum company's new extrusion plant.

DOUGLAS LePAN

METAGYMNASTICS

1

Raise both your ideas upwards
   Now
      keeping your life straight
lean towards doubt
      Stretch   Stretch further
If you do it right
   you should feel the tension in your belief
Go as far as you can   Pause
   Now bring your ideas upwards
Incline steadily towards the good
   keeping your life straight
If you do it right
     you'll notice
   how evil presses on your thought

2

Ready?
   Good and evil each side of your god
Now raise your thought slowly
   keeping your doubt straight
   Look along your belief
   making sure your head is erect
Then
   turning your eyes towards death
bend your doubt
   until belief and thought are just touching
Try not to stiffen

3

Lie on your death
   Breathe deeply   Hold!
Look at your god
   Expire through your life
Repeat a few times   Rest

Then
>   both ideas fully extended
raise your doubts
>   moving your evil backwards
>   till you feel a tingling sensation
>   in your good
Close your eyes   Relax

4

Ideas together
stretch your belief out in front
bending your thought
till it points vertically upwards
>   Do the same with your doubt
Then
>   press your thought and doubt together
>   till you feel your life contracting
Pause   Relax the pressure
You can repeat this several times
Then
>   swing thought and doubt outwards
Stretch them as far as you can
>   Relax   And at the end
>   >   breathe deeply

5

You'll need a long belief for this one
>   Spring on to it
>   >   getting a good purchase with both ideas
When you feel sure
swing your doubt upwards
>   and let your good grasp it firmly
Death down
>   flex your life
>   till evil and doubt
>   >   are directly under your belief
You should find that life and death
are now just touching

Now
    head between ideas
you should be able
        to just raise your good
(Practice improves)   Pause
Now return to your first position
Exhale deeply
And always breathe deeply through your life.

                NOEL MACAINSH

YOUNG DELINQUENT

Pushed from his mother's lap too early
So that another member of the team
Can have his too brief innings, he collects
His playmates from the street as easily
As hands and knees get dirt, and a few yards
Of gritty pavement form his only playground.

With a few broken toys, tin cans and bricks
He fabricates a world to stretch his mind
And makes the nearest wall his Everest.

After school roaming near the river
He jumps a lorry rumbling from the docks
With other boys, fumbles beneath the sheets
And finds a treasure trove of fruit or nuts,
Sugar or chocolate . . . and trespasses
On railway cuttings trapping wild rock-pigeons
To keep in back-yard boxes . . . tests his skill
Climbing a warehouse wall, chancing his luck . . .
And on that instant's stamped a criminal.

By casual peccadilloes of the street
He moves through nursery stages into crime.
Police files record his long delinquency;
Magistrates probe and ponder on his case.
He takes his cue and cons his given part,
Learning his role which is to break the rule.

But no one anywhere breaks in with love,
Or makes a simple reconciling move!
The play proceeds—a small domestic farce—
Watched by bored officers, baffled social workers,
And social scientists making case-studies,
Minds stuffed with aetiologies and theories
All evanescing in a cloud of words,

THE MOTH-HAND

Bruised and white,
the moth-hand flutters toward the light-
switch, transparent as gauze.
Immune to my critical eye, it has no shame,
is what it is,
seems to have no memory of what it was.
I cannot say the same.

I cannot believe
that the hand can gather its strength to move
after all it's been through.
I watch it as one would watch
a crippled war hero stripping in public,
trying pathetically to recapture attention
the only way he knows how.

I think of the hand's women,
of its features memorized line by line,
its fingers lingering along the lips
of a mouth half open, half closed,
or separating the soft chambers of love.
I remember when its every movement seemed
quick or angry or emphatic or furtive.

Now we are like lovers
who have quarreled—not once but over and over
until the issue is impossible to distinguish.
I try to think what it might mean.
But the light clicks off, and the moth-hand
glows for a long moment,
sizzling in its one wish.

GARY MIRANDA

TO ISABEL WHO HID IN MY CLOSET IN BUENOS AIRES ON CHRISTMAS DAY, ON CHRISTMAS DAY

I found you there, knees tucked up
like the elf they hang on Christmas trees,
in your pink orphan's uniform and your brown eyes.

I found you there
trapped between my trousers and my shoes.
Trapped between ages:
old enough to try and try well;
too young to see the folly of the plan.

As if I *could* take you with me.
As if when the ship sailed you would be safe.
Forever.
As if my home were anywhere that Argentina wasn't,
a place that walled no children in,
a fortress against time.

You spoke in Spanish, sobbing,
and I did not understand —
which is to say, I did,
but turned you in anyway:
to the other world, the real one,
to adults who run the orphanage,
the proper authorities.

You return, Isabel: on off days;
in the faces of children in Valparaiso;
in the black mirror on the back of my closet door
where I crouch in a darkness of my own.
Waiting.

GARY MIRANDA

THE THIRTEENTH YEAR

1

Far from us,
the boys with water up to their knees
were dreaming girls and open lotus gardens.
They kept the oxen's thick breath
in the right wind
and were keen to the crocodiles
when they made the water glide
between the reeds.

I saw their yellow faces the first time
in my apartment. I had a drink in one hand.
The air was cooled to 70°.
I saw their yellow faces the second time
when we landed. I had a knife
heavy on my leg, a gun in a leather-shaped
heart-shaped case over my heart.
The air must have been 120°.
The heat brought little bones
to the surface of their skin
and made their lips open and die dry.

Water and heat were over the dock
when I saw the brown breasts
of the dreaming girls.
Through the unbuttoned shirts
they opened like fine flowers.

2

I flew the mountains
high and green and the widening water
out to sea. Far under us
the boys tunneled in the earth.
On their bellies they waited for the
silent encounter that was crawling
up the mountain.

Leaf and bird had the teeth of crocodiles
and the water gliding over the ledge
covered the snipers' advance.
The crack of a twig was a flaming dream.
In the open lotus the girls were still pungent.
I flew the mountains high and red
and the thick water widening out to sea.

Far under us
the boys were silent as prayers
in the gold pagodas.
They had shaved their heads.
They had forgotten how to dream
but in their white sheets were trying
to penetrate the dead. Sweat and ash.
The incense went over their skulls
in invisible explosions.
They were certain of the right wind
and gasoline blossomed in their pores.
Sweat and ash.

3

I got a week-end pass from the base
and traveled to the capital.
I went to bars where police
and soldiers quarreled over liquor
and women were for the asking.
I followed a dark girl
through the back streets of the city.
We bought a white sweet bag and lay down.
The water was gliding under our curved backs.
We smoked a hundred blooming fields.

Far from us in Da Nang
the jungles turned shower to flame
and tigers were incinerated in one leap.
Flesh perforated like black orchids

and death had a tropic odor.
In Quang Tri centuries of dynasty
buckled at the knees,
soldiers' blood ran down palace walls,
and the walls went down
into the earth.

We smoked a hundred blooming fields
and the water gliding under our curved backs.

In the Mekong Delta
the enemy multiplied like rice,
their small brown heads moving
in waves over the land.
Crocodiles stretched their jaws
and their huge bellies slid off the banks.

Needles and triggers
were fixed in their fingers
when I saw their yellow faces
for the last time.

Sweat and ash.
The air must have been 120°.
I flew the ocean high and green
though the sweet sap
was thickening in my veins.
The air must have been 70°.

GLENN MORAZZINI

WALLACE STEVENS' LETTERS

I never wanted fifty-five to happen.
How many times I turned back to the pages
where, green before us, lay the early fifties
in ambience of constant understatement.

I never wanted summer to be on us.
I kept backtracking to the longer letters,
hoping those mild, clear, Hartford summer evenings
might last forever, need not come to this.

I kept delaying that year in my mind,
kept putting off that logical succession
which had brought me lovingly to the fire
insisting that its name be spelled completion.

I wanted that, each night, leaving the office,
he stop at Dean's and carry home a plum cake,
sleep with the windows open, bring back mangoes
from those trips to New York, a clear Meursault.

I wanted Dean's never to close or move,
open its doors on Sundays, after midnight,
should the baker see his form at the window
and hurry from the back room to admit him.

I kept resisting summer's blinding progress,
wanted July to blossom without end,
those dominations of wind, work, and weather,
Hartford to be where one most wished to be.

I wanted pictures still to come from Paris,
Ceylon never to waver sending tea.
I wanted that José write from Havana
weather is as you like it: unrelenting.

I kept hoping Knopf would postpone the volume
which he attempted, each year, not to think of,
one that he most feared would be called Collected,
knowing it sounded much too final for him.

Reality, of couse, was what he wanted,
a Cuban burro, night to be the night.
I wanted not reprieve but prolongation,
Connecticut immaculate with light.

I drew the palaz cloud-capped, visionary;
I painted Hoon's magnificence and sweep.
I never wanted desolation's silence.
I needed the alternatives to speak.

I never wanted what, in time, would happen;
I never meant for night to fall so deep.
Astonishments, I wanted you unstinting.
Sea-surfaces, I dreamt you running sweet.

I pictured the Comedian a juggler,
Tehuantepec by mythic waters lapped.
Each night I hear the music going under,
Key West too darkly singing on the map.

HERBERT MORRIS

SEALS AT HIGH ISLAND

for Emily

The calamity of seals begins with jaws.
Born in caverns that reverberate
With endless malice of the sea's tongue
Clacking on shingle, they learn to bark back
In fear and sadness and celebration.
The ocean's mouth opens forty feet wide
And closes on a morsel of their rock.

Swayed by the thrust and backfall of the tide,
A dappled grey bull and a brindled cow
Copulate in the green water of a cove.
I watch from a cliff-top, trying not to move.
Sometimes they sink and merge into black shoals;
Then rise for air, his muzzle on her neck,
Their winged feet intertwined as a fish-tail.

She opens her fierce mouth like a scarlet flower
Full of white seeds; she holds it open long
At the sunburst in the music of their loving;
And cries a little. But I must remember
How far their feelings are from mine marooned.
If there are tears at this holy ceremony
Theirs are caused by brine and mine by breeze.

When the great bull withdraws his rod, it glows
Like a carnelian candle set in jade.
The cow ripples ashore to feed her calf;
While an old rival, eyeing the deed with hate,
Swims to attack the tired triumphant god.
They rear their heads above the boiling surf,
Their terrible jaws open, jetting blood.

At nightfall they haul out, and mourn the drowned,
Playing to the sea sadly their last quartet,
An improvised requiem that ravishes
Reason, while ripping scale up like a net:
Brings pity trembling down the rocky spine
Of headlands, till the bitter ocean's tongue
Swells in their cove, and smothers their sweet song.

      RICHARD MURPHY

THE FLYING MURAL

It was all vivid. The Southern Cross passed M. Blériot
And his rain-squall-cooled engine. A red Fokker conjured the Luftwaff
Wings creaked over oceans, Lindbergh chasing them sideways
The Flying Doctor aligned on folklore's two-legged windsock.

It was death and adventure. The interruptor gear fired through it.
Even when bombs screamed Guernica, and Rotterdammed Europe
And more than Europe, it sparkled. The rotors shoaled upward.
Boys worshipped SAC and June Allyson, beta rays in their bones.

And then it sagged. Even as paddies doused napalm
And robots, of flesh and metal, impinged on the moon
The records were fading to paper, the Boeings to buses
And people were starting again to dream of flying.

The painter sat close to tears. The wall he had worked
Was a river of surface bearing his clean wings away.
The machines shaped like power and prayer had lost that balance
Deeply. It was all mastery, and all mastered.

Greying men praised piston fighters: *They were the sweetest
Bone meat of man's estrangement. We outflew it in them.*
But boys rose into the sky, heads sheeted in flame
And the ruined ones dived on sitting-rooms worse than on mills.

In that strange time, the painter started trying
Many things on the air: wheels, mountains, picnic parties,
The underside of ploughing; shares like reversed steel fins
Streamed the furrow layer. And then he depicted the dead

With silver faces, and broke though on wisdom. He made them
Mix with the living in all the streets of that weather
Forgiving and boasting. The living asked questions and cried.
Men wiring a rocket stage looked up, sensing something.

but even their ground was bound by unravelling winds
to the great earth herself, the flyer among flyers.
Only the forceful and the despairing people
now bet on the wall being thick, opaque or endless

and not a surface for art (there is no other)
the everywhere door of the dead, and love's sheer standard.
The planet was worked with cities and oceans and stems
and though on a globe, the fields rose and fell, with horizons

So wonderful was the workmanship. I saw children
planting out delicate seedlings to learn engineering.
Steel and acanthus were longing to marry again.
A man in that city worked on growth-rate figures

somewhere between these and the earliest weapon, he said
is the Enemy. We thought he had holed up in incest —
a dead airman told him *Watch out for the hun in the Sun.*
The painter's brush danced like the spirit of detachment

and its every touch was a human figure of calm
free readiness, at the meeting place of now wings.
Here I went into the wall, the dimensionless judgement.
The last I saw of the foothold earth, it was flying,

A faithful Dakota, a vibrant Spad, a royal Zeppelin
with its Walrus islands and scuffed Friendship towns
on sidereal course, the sun on its upper ice planes,
stunting Hercules-ward at some immense but not ravenous

speed that might silver its colours off. The bombs
in its concrete bays were dying of power and stance
but those who praised Udet and Hinkler, they glittered like grains.
I went with no ripcord and was among friends forever.

Les A. Murray

PLANTS

While conducting experiments to make spineless cacti I often talked to the plants to create a vibration of love. "You have nothing to fear," I would tell them.
—Luther Burbank

It is not only light, moisture, and warm earth
they respond to, but also kindness and love.
I have always suspected they were like that.
For I know they make love. I have seen them
doing it.
        They cling to each other
or wave suggestive arms (pansies even make
love to themselves). They stiffen
and throw their seeds hard
against the ground, rubbing their thin bodies
up against each other promiscuously.

Milkweed testicles seed the wind. They take off
conspicuous things and drop their blooms
permissively, turning their buds inside out
to show us perfumed vulvae and sweet depths.

Just watch them do *that* sometime, greatly speeded up
on film, and tell me you are not aroused!
Ripe clefts of pink, red, yellow, blue—pulsing
buds and ticking ovaries. Tender undersides.
Erected stamens listen to the wind.

Exhibitionists all! Young Ted Roethke learned
these things watching them for hours. Thought
they were obscene.
                But they are not
always loving; they can be deadly.
For instance at night in hospitals
they are not allowed alone with some patients.

Moreover they donate themselves lavishly
to our deaths. Forget-me-nots smile ironically
on our graves.
                    Do they talk to each other?
We cut them, but they cannot cry out when it hurts.
Or can they? Maybe they can
only tell the others. Then they too are frightened
and lean back thinking it their turn next.

I know we need them. Still I wonder how much
we hurt them. And late at night they lean toward
our reading lamps to listen, or press their noses
against our window panes.
                         O what might they do
some day in way of retaliation?
They have their underground: daffodils, hyacinths,
tulips, potatoes. Strawberries send their runners out.
Raspberries put their ears to the ground
and listen to the telegraph plants.

Perhaps some day we will wake up
to flytraps, spines, creepers, choking
vines and loco weed grown perfect
as the fly amanita and belladonna nightshade.

                         MICHAEL NIFLIS

A NEW LEAF

I look forward to next year's diary
In which your name will not appear.
The lamp you gave me is broken,
The sheets have been laundered
And yesterday I woke, made tea
And shaved before remembering
That you were dead.

The healing process has begun
And what mends first is flesh.
Some veterans of World War One
Go round with shrapnel
Lodged in them like pips. The body
Puts itself together. Tissue knits,
But nothing is the same.

I feel grief like a stitch
In the side, sense it like a missing stair.
You are safe in the context of time;
There's a before and after,
But in between I see you still:
Your heavy breasts, your waist tobogganing
Into a bank of bone, your cockled toes,
Your hair spilling like water.

You are printed on me
Like a leaf in stone, a transfer
Of what's gone. Your absence
Has an outline and I conform to it.
My blood runs down the gulley
Of your signature; we walk in step,
Profile to profile. With my eyes open
Or shut I read you like braille.

I can forget dates, anniversaries:
Your recollected face already looks
Less like your photograph.
But in the dark-room of my mind the series
Endlessly extends, editions multiply.

No diary can keep you out.
You fill each empty page, cancelling time,
Making your mark again, again, again,
Raging with love against the day
That dares to post you missing.

PHILIP OAKES

SEIZURE

and you are gone

outside the window sparrows cascade upward
your neighbor, in an old jacket, is trudging to the river
where the sun flies off the banked-up ice
and the spicy-green stinging-green heads of mallards
and behind you the house is right-angled, perfect
as constructed things can be perfect

sunlight broken by windowpanes falls slantwise
in your seizure
light manic pounding that is not a metaphor

at the center of your body
the body not a metaphor
and breath goes shallow, swift, choppy with cunning
to get you through
not a metaphor for breath but breath
breath itself needing to be intelligent

outside, there is breathing
it is all breathing calmly
the turbulence of the birds is their breathing
their souls emerge like that, in spurts of noise
the constant bobbing of the ducks, dipping
the waves caressing them roughly
out where the half-dozen yards of raw ice
breathes into the river

thoughts rise in you in quick darts
the thoughts you recall from the last seizure
needing to stand like this, paralyzed,
in a timeless time
where the center of your body is unfriendly
and you need to think

*dying now in a house of right-angled perfections
a borrowed celebration of sunshine and birds
how good, how ordinary—*

take it as a gift

but the body sweats with panic
cannot believe a stray death is so easy
cannot believe it is always yourself
surrendered to that breathing

JOYCE CAROL OATES

HYSTERECTOMY IN MUNICH

They pry her mouth open.
My sister is gassed.
This operation has been done before.
Records will be properly kept.
While she flies a Klieg light
over a peagreen sea
the surgeon gives orders.
A stainless West German
knife sinks in her belly.
Blood grows
like time-lapsed poppies.

Across the city
twin phalluses
of Frauenkirche
maintain their erections
as for five centuries.
At Nuremberg Stadium
her friends cheer
a rock group.
The surgeon paints
sterile cotton
bright carnelian.
He is a hummingbird
x-ing his needlepoint.
Tissue drops into
plastic bags.
She rides a slab
to the recovery room

where she climbs back
with lead bells chained
to both ankles
with staples punched
in her tear.

Over her head
a Bavarian moon
opens its mouth.
Two Bavarian dumplings
sway above her
and though she is free,
white, and twenty
she cries for the room
for the language
for the mother
she has cut away.

    CAROLE OLES

THE FAMILY

The dark things of the wood
Are coming from their caves,
Flexing muscle.

They browse the orchard,
Nibble the sea of grasses
Around our yellow rooms,

Scarcely looking in
To see what we are doing
And if they still know us.

We hear them, or think we do:
The muzzle lapping moonlight,
The tooth in the apple.

Put another log on the fire;
Mozart, again, on the turntable.
Still there is a sorrow

With us in the room.
We remember the cave.
In our dreams we go back

Or they come to visit.
They also like music.
We eat leaves together.

They are our brothers.
They are the family
We have run away from.

MARY OLIVER

PRUNING FRUIT TREES

Begin by cutting
all branches away
that are now dead.
It is March. One surely feels
in the air a softness
that has not yet arrived.
The cut must be made close
to the parent limb
following the angle
of its growth.
Used snow inches deep shows
yesterday's boot-prints,
my son's and mine, circling
each other, circling each tree.
Where two equal branches
now divide, choose one and cut—
it is not good that they contend
for vital sap.
The cut must be made close
to the parent limb,
soon it will smoothly heal.
The chickadees scold us;
by their feeder, they have their rights.
Don't be afraid to cut—that's it,
cut more, it's good for the tree,
lengthening life,
making its fruit full.
A farmer told me to talk
to the trees. Tell them
"this is good for you."
Speak softly. Thank them.
It is June. Our footprints faintly
circle the trees in the moist grass.
Like little berries, the fruit is hard.
They will make it, they will hold on.

See, they will hold on, they will ripen,
they will do well.
It is June. I have learned
to ask for nothing more.
I have never
been happier than this.
Tell them they will do well.
As wind flutters their leaves,
praise them.
It is March. The cut
must be made close
to the parent limb.

ROBERT PACK

MOTION AND REST

When the maenads murdered and dismembered Orpheus
Because he refused their god and preached Helios
Apollo from the Thracian hill and spoke against
Ritual killing,

His limbs were scattered but they threw his head
Into the river Hebrus and as it drifted down
The long stream, through mountainous country, uncut
Cedars and hemlocks,

Sheer outcrops, thickets tangled with ivy,
Banks where the blue-flag iris blossomed,
Where moss-deer shadowed the water, the head of
Orpheus, singing

Toward Lesbos, held out in a constant moment
All that he was: his song recounted
Animal enchantments, the inward life-force
Of trees and fountains,

The sweetness of the flesh, the stunned silence
Of the gods of death, the impossible consent,
The steep return, the bitter struggle with
Himself and the negative

Pull back down from the sun-filled cave-mouth
To eternal darkness. The flowing water
Was transparent as his song and although it took him
Into unknown country,

Altered times, though it threatened to silence
His forecast on disenchanted rocks, Orpheus
Sang in the lips of his song and his music was
Glamorous, charming,

Unreflective as the cedars and hemlocks, the sheer
Outcrops drenched in sunlight, the banks
Where the blue-flag iris blossoms and moss-deer
Shadow the water.

      RICHARD PEVEAR

HIGH FREQUENCY

They say that trees scream
under the bulldozer's blade.
That when you give it water,
the potted coleus sings.
Vibrations quiver about leaves
our ears are too gross
to comprehend.

Yet I hear on this street
where sprinklers twirl
on exterior carpeting
a high rising whine.
That grass looks wellfed.
It must come from inside
where a woman on downs is making
a creative environment
for her child.

The spring earth cracks
above germinating seeds.
Hear that subliminal roar,
a wind through grass and skirts,
the sound of hair crackling,
the slither of anger
just surfacing.

Pressed against glass and yellowing,
scrawny, arching up to the
insufficient light, plants
that do not belong in houses
sing of what they want:

like a woman who's been told
she can't carry a tune,
like a woman afraid people will laugh

if she raises her voice,
like a woman whose veins surface
compressing a scream,
like a woman whose mouth hardens
to hold locked in her own
harsh and beautiful song.

                        Marge Piercy

WINTER '72

for Kevin

Low under the crook of the hill
snugged away in your sea room house
we come together crewlike and contented
with the whole unwholesome host of our fantasies

outside and above the boiling cove
above the age-old fish-storied stages
(resisting still in their trembling old age
the never-say-die seaweeded sea)
the sky crawling gulls claw
at the white confusion of the whistling wind
scratch their screeching frenzy
on the impenetrable windwall of our alliance

cozied now in the elbow of your armchair
I perceive the corrupting blue day's dawn
creeping like cats into your seaside yard
and curling comfortable in the lap of your living room
consider time's timeless quarrel
with the poor ever orphaned earth

within this room this wishedfor dawnless day
the only colors are those of my own invention
like you yourself sitting stone blue
behind the veiled blueness of your cigarette smoke
curling now like cobras
about your martyred head
like me sitting as colorless
as a decomposed king
wishing for you a spangled princess
sprawled weeping among her veils
begging your forgiveness

like this house brown and burlapped
like a cocoon from which we will uncurl
when thankgod daylight breaks
and splinters the stained sea windows
releasing us weak-winged
into the salty and seagulled sky

AL PITTMAN

IDENTITIES

He thinks he knows a little about love.
A river-bank, the branches crowding round,
Imprisoning the sun, the yellow leaves
Embracing, wilting slightly in the heat;
Those stream-smooth pebbles, lying just too deep
To reach. The sound of water in the hills,
A vacant summer evening closing in,
The darkening grass, the branches vanishing.
Watching his mirror-image watching him
Behind the bar, he almost loves himself.

Almost. And yet his mind is following
A cloud across a birdless winter sky,
Or prints set hard in snow, or passages
Through leafless woods. The geometric trees
Do not embrace: they touch, scratch, and unfold
The wounds of winter, the futility
Of making contact. Best to stand and drink
Secure in some bright apathetic world;
To wait, and hope someone will penetrate
His abstract code, but still not understand.

It is an old accepted paradox,
Escape's vague border with reality.
He needs a bar, an image, and a pose
To which the moss of solitude will cling.
He turns and says, "The counterpoint of Bach
Is like that of the Modern Jazz Quartet
But not so brittle." Living in an age
Of jagged noises and too brittle sounds,
We choose either the wilted summer leaf
Or else the branches' patterned skeleton.

He thinks of blind men, tries to share the lack
Of image crushed upon the retina:

They have their perfect vision, not the sight
Of years or days or placid winter skies;
Yet he retains the fading vestiges,
The summers and the fallings out of love.
He chooses winter, treading where the fox
Has trod, where rabbits ran some other day,
And where the tracks are frozen hard. He thinks
He knows too little and too much of love.

NEIL POWELL

CRYSTAL

A man wets his forefinger with his tongue and holds
up a perfect water glass, empty and glistening.
He is sitting at a table in a large
hall with other men in identical blue

blazers with eagle medallions over their breast pockets.
Now the first man fingers the glass
rim, tentatively, as if it were jagged-edged.
And now he strokes it clockwise, slowly, stopping

to wet his finger again and again, like an old
man paging through a book—until the glass comes
to life with a thin, high whine like nothing
he has ever heard, and the others look up in amazement, catching

on, holding up their glasses, too, wetting and stroking
them clockwise like ice skaters in unison.
All the glasses are coming to life now; their throats are
slowly catching fire, glistening with a thinner,

higher whine than any bird. It is like a pitch
pipe with wings. It is something like the music each
man heard when he stepped outside at night
for the first time alone as a boy. Then

there was nothing in the sky but stars and music.
And the sky was like glass.

JAMES REISS

THE BREATHERS

Jeffrey Andrew Reiss—October 5, 1969

In Ohio, where these things happen,
we had been loving all winter.
By June you looked down and saw your belly
was soft as fresh bread.

In Florida, standing on the bathroom
scales, you were convinced—
and looked both ways for a full minute before crossing
Brickell Boulevard.

In Colorado you waited-out summer in a mountain
cabin, with Dr. Spock,
your stamps, and my poems in the faint
8,000-foot air.

> Listen, he had a perfect body,
> right down to his testicles, which I counted.
> The morning he dropped from your womb, all rosy
> as an apple in season, breathing the thick
> fall air of Ohio, we thought good things would happen.

> Believe me, Dr. Salter and the nurses were right:
> he was small but feisty—they said he was
> *feisty*. That afternoon in his respirator
> when he urinated it was something to be proud of.
> Cyanotic by evening, he looked like a dark rose.

Late that night you hear. . . .

> Think of the only possible twentieth century consolations:
> Doris saying it might have been better this way.
> Think of brain damage, car crashes, dead soldiers:
> better seventeen hours than eighteen, twenty years
> of half-life in Ohio where nothing happens.

Late that night you hear them
in the....

    For, after all, we are young, traveling
    at full speed into the bull's eye of the atom.
    There's a Pepsi-and-hot-dog stand in that bull's eye,
    and babies of the future dancing around us.
    Listen, the air is thick with our cries!

Late that night you hear them
in the nursery, the breathers.
Their tiny lungs go in and out like the air
bladder on an oxygen tank
or the rhythm of sex.
Asleep, your arms shoot towards that target
with a stretch that lifts you like a zombie,
wakes you to the deafening breathers.
And now you see them, crawling
rings around your bed, in blankets,
buntings, preemies in incubators circling
on casters, a few with cleft palates, heart trouble,
all feistily breathing, crawling
away from your rigidly outstretched arms—
breathing, robbing the air.

                                                                                                         JAMES REISS

FROM A SURVIVOR

The pact that we made was the ordinary pact
of men & women in those days

I don't know who we thought we were
that our personalities
could resist the failures of the race

Lucky or unlucky, we didn't know
the race had failures of that order
and that we were going to share them

Like everybody else, we thought of ourselves as special

Your body is as vivid to me
as it ever was: even more

since my feeling for it is clearer:
I know what it could do & could not do

it is no longer
the body of a god
or anything with power over my life

Next year it would have been 20 years
and you are wastefully dead
who might have made the leap
we talked, too late, of making

which I live now
not as a leap
but a succession of brief, amazing movements

each one making possible the next

Adrienne Rich

MARRIAGE COUNSEL

Your problem is not unusual
Indeed its absence would be that.
(Regard this room as a confessional,
Nothing you tell me will leak out.)
So far, it seems, your principal trouble
Is your wife's indifference, her failure to hear
Whenever you speak, in bed or at table,
Her remote and unrecording stare.
These are not uncommon features of marriage,
In fact the contrary would be true.
You suspect an urgent need for copulation
With an unknown some-one, the opposite of you?
She puts black stuff round her eyes, and wears
Unaccustomed underclothes,
Ambiguous, weightless as mist? She dyes
The grey bits of her hair and shows
A strange new taste for vulgar romantic songs?
None of this need suggest another man.
You say she has never had strong lungs
Yet, despite Government Health-Warnings, she has begun
To smoke cigarettes — expensive, King-size.
It may be the menopause, although
Her new vocabulary might give cause
For perturbation. It could show
That she is being refashioned utterly,
Which certainly suggests a mentor, a new friend.
In this case you must try to be
A different person too. It need not be the end.
Re-woo her. Win her hand again.
And if you fail — which might well occur —
This reflection should ease the ensuing pain:
Consider. You will not really have lost her
Because, from all you say, she is other
Than the woman you married. She is remade.
In this case you have never possessed her
And cannot therefore be betrayed.

Later, the former, the familiar wife
May return. It has often happened before.
But, if she does, do not expect life
To be suddenly charged with honeyed splendour
And harmonious chords. You must not be surprised
If you find your need and passion are dead.
There are times when defeat is to be prized
Above victory.
                          Good day to you. You will forget all
                                              I have said.

                              VERNON SCANNELL

WHERE SHALL WE GO?

Waiting for her in the usual bar
He finds she's late again.
Impatience frets at him,
But not the fearful, half-sweet pain he knew
So long ago.

That cherished perturbation is replaced
By styptic irritation
And, under that, a cold
Dark current of dejection moves
That this is so.

There was a time when all her failings were
Delights he marvelled at :
It seemed her clumsiness,
Forgetfulness and wild non-sequiturs
Could never grow

Wearisome, nor would he ever tire
Of doting on those small
Blemishes that proved
Her beauty as the blackbird's gloss affirms
The bridal snow.

The clock above the bar records her theft
Of time he cannot spare ;
Then suddenly she's there.
He stands to welcome and accuse her with
A grey hello.

And sees, for one sly instant, in her eyes
His own aggrieved dislike
Wince back at him before
Her smile draws blinds. "Sorry I'm late," she says.
"Where shall we go ?"

      Vernon Scannell

CARNIVAL GAMES

So you're gone.
With your reasons floating behind like banners,
some tacky color, pink or chartreuse.
With your reasons ringing like bells
against this wash of night you've left me to.
Gone like a magician flicking doves to the air.
They crash against my windows.
They tangle in my hair.
A Houdini, you've escaped from too much love.
But wait: this light I'll make
will spin night into darkness you'll remember
past all your carnival music, past that lacy mask you trail.
While the flares march by outside,
while you dance between them,
there's one thing you've forgot:
we're all magicians,
all.

Come watch my work.
I'll swallow these first like hard candy:
red, yellow, white: they crunch against my heart,
little tambourine bells, then turn time-bombs.
They're flashing rainbow signals!
Eight, nine, ten: I leave this note,
and not for love or hate,
but for my own good name,
because my witchcraft works,
because I want to leave you right.
Red, yellow, white: they're fireworks you'll be missing.

Come warm your hands above my bed.
Unsay those words, a backwards spell.
Kneel to this light before I break,
all jewels and splendour.
Bring a big brass band!
Before day comes,

I'll be the last one dancing,
The Queen of Mardi Gras,
and then I'll vanish
better oh better than you.
You'll never find me.

    JESSIE SCHELL

AGORAPHOBIA

From this distance, my eyes well
shaded by the deep trees, I can see
the danger they're in, those
                            people down there, alone,
in the middle of that huge bank
of the Russian River, where Austin Creek
flows into it.
               A boat, a chair,
a camper the woman is staring into,
one hand holding the back door open, thinking
what to cook for supper.
                    The man
on his spine in a patio chair, hip
boots, hat down over his eyes, open chest
of tackle alongside, & two rods.
                         The child
squatting by the beached aluminum boat skipping
stones across the thin water.
                    I can see
the danger. They have wandered la-de-da
into that open zone. They have driven their camper
with all their lashed gear & belongings
down onto, out into that enormous field. They are
without
          protection. Don't they know
that the unending December sky can't see them?
That it's up there with such immensity
that a fleet of Ford Camper Trucks, of Ward's
Lite-Wate Six Foot Fishers, all fully equipped,
with crowds of humanity to match would fall
equally dead center of the sky's blindness?
                               Can't they see
that that vast dry bank belongs to the flood to come?
That even a naked man in a desert stands no chance?

What's the matter with those people?
                          From where I sit,
they seem propped in the dark of something so empty, so
killing, so inhuman, I want to
                          cry out, warn them. We need
something to redeem our desolation,
some counter-immensity, some enemy-space we can
pit against this emptiness.
                 Or I would
have us all stones. Here & now. Us
& all our belongings turned into stones.
Stones in the dry rivers.
Stones in the bellies of fishes.
Stones in the deepest trenches of the oceans. Stones
heavy as planets yielding finally
to the anti-gravity of the sky.

                         DONALD SCHENKER

THE SHELLS

A guided tour in the Andes

These shells are from no familiar sea—
they litter furrows in the mountain fields.
Ploughing turns them over year to year.
They come back more predictably than maize:

almost ordinary, like a worker's bruised nails,
but inside luminous in certain lights
as mother pearl. They are stone now. The plough
can chip them but they are the years':

they do not break outright.
When these mountains were lifted from the sea
they carried the live cities of the sea—
the scallop beds, the clams in families

fisted onto marl, and sand a pure
salt white. The water rilled away; the salts
have worked their passage back to water.
The shells stayed until they are these stones

among farmers who have never seen the sea
or tasted fish, who plough with wood
and weed by hand and touch them as elaborate
queer flints or coloured stones.

This is what time does when history
leaves it to itself—retrieves organic
monuments for a longer eternity than ours—
these mute informers that are twice over

stone: of memory and stone. We might
stop here a day and gather them
as Darwin did in sacks, to ship home
for minute interrogation. We might spend

an hour with the Indian farmers
to whom we are enigmas, rich and pale,
and tell them how the fine-lipped shells,
the delicate bright eyes of soil are not

real stone, how these coarse fields
plunder a dead sea city that—
if they knew its language—
could rob them of their given catechism.

Better leave them be, each to his field,
ploughing securely towards their Seventh Day.
We have our own sufficient luggage
of broken promises and curios for home.

The bus is ready and our tribe is tired.
We'll keep a secret they could not believe
and let the shells be turned and turned for seasons
as the unspent coins of passage out of faith.

       MICHAEL SCHMIDT

SHEEP

As they would come,
they lit up the distance
like rocks at dusk;
the low bagpipe
of their voices
filling the afternoon,
flowing over its brim
into the center
of the field.

Sheep, with a common failing,
they knew each other
and that was all:
perfect victims
that the dogs
could tease,
as helpless, one
by one, as clouds.

Seeing them at sundown,
tight against each other
like some freezing
arctic infantry,
they move,
a single beast, looking
foolish as they
plunge against the dark,
against the imperfect
scent of wolves,
whipping them to run..

They seem demented
in their following,
slaves to a law
invisible to all but them,

going over waterfalls
in its service,
dead in canyons
at the foot of cliffs.

Dead sheep: voiceless,
inexplicable
to men who never
saw their priesthood
and devotions;
saw how passionate
dumb beasts can be,
saving the appearances,
fearing the teeth and claws
of the active, silent
blank.

   LEROY SEARLE

ANOTHER DARKNESS

when I stay awake all night
for whatever purpose
morning accuses me
of a new understanding of absence

another dawn arrives
as if I had been waiting for it
and the mountains approach
looking blue and innocent
trying to convince me
they were standing there all the time
when I know they were somewhere else
staring into another darkness

tiny crystals of ice
form while I'm not looking and depart
before I can tell them goodby
how difficult
to live on such a schedule

darkness
place without maps
place without encumbrances
can I lay claim to your country
whose trees bear no initials

RICHARD SHELTON

SONORA FOR SALE

this is the land of gods in exile
they are fragile and without pride
they require no worshippers

we come down a white road in the moonlight
dragging our feet like innocents
to find the guilty already arrived
and in possession of everything

we see the stars as they were years ago
but for us it is the future
they warn us too late

we are here we cannot turn back
soon we hold out our hands
full of money
this is the desert
it is all we have left to destroy

RICHARD SHELTON

ARARAT

Somebody said the sea would come to us
cutting like an army through wheat—
its captive women, dolphins in the wake
of our little boat. As water drains
every wife's a sea-wife. Such traffic
you would think it market day!
Hooked to their elbows, baskets
of apricots and limes
anchor the widows in the muddy slopes
where the world begins. The elements
have never been more married.

I have grown to love tending this garden
that barks and coos in the moonlight
when there is a moon.
Spindly giraffes cluster at the bow.
Ants inch down the plank in twos.
The sheep are nervous. Their thick wool
steams as the dew burns off.

Crises crush men more. In sleep
my husband's pitchy hands hammer the air
as if another boat could float us back
to who we were. I imagine
I am the mountain he teeters on
as every wave of wind comes past.
I watch for clouds.

JANE SHORE

JOURNEYS AND CHANGES

I and the man with the pinto pig
Walked the shore at high mid-day:
She snorted and snuffled and rooted among
                        The sand-dunes and seashells

Looking, perhaps, for truffles; bounding
Away from the waves, then gingerly wading
Hock-deep, no more, distrusting the thrust of her
                        Delicate hooves.

Engrossed among pebbles we talked of the distance
Between sty and beach, measured in hoof-lengths,
Stones'-throws and yard-sticks, thumbnails and axeheads,
                        Inch-worms and parsecs.

Sties and beaches, journeys and changes.
Dolphins footsore in the salt marshes
Sliding back to the stinging cold surf
                        And forests of Ocean

Journeys. Lungfish leaving behind
The breathless water to wander across
A sun-cracked mudflat, bound to exchange
                        One slough for another.

And we crushed some seashells to chalk on our fingers
Thinking of creatures born into aimlessness
Casing themselves in layers of armor
                        As we have used words.

And we spoke of men, who at last walk erect
Through the blazing galaxy; mushroom-headed and
Crooked of back, sowing the Moon
                        For towers and radishes.

We walked, we three, two miles and back
Politely evading the sidling gulls.
Her lashes bleached and her skin turned pink
        Around its dapples.

And coming back we made her a garland
(which she ignored) of cat-tails and bamboo,
Daisies and skate-eggs, weed-pods and beach-roses
        Plaited together.

And watching her amble, trailing her flowers,
Politely evading the sidling gulls,
We laughed at the burdens we'd loaded upon her
        Under the sun
               Between sty and sea.

                        Robert L. Smith

NOW THE SLOW CREATION

Now the slow creation of things
comes everywhere:
the warm lapping of petals
in the sun; the leaf that turns
its sitcky surface to the air.

Slowly, my pocket opens like an orange,
warm to your touch;
and that five-petaled sun
folds all its fruited segments out.
I turn forever on that bed.

And out of that arc, delicately rising,
children swim like fish
or seahorses; thistle-slim,
their bellies bent,
into the new-rinsed light.

Who put them there, you put
them there, marvelously fat-fingered.
A great soft whoosh of the breath—
they come, endlessly spinning
like soap bubbles through a pipe.

KATHLEEN SPIVACK

MR. D.

I think of you sometimes, how you came.
You were in brown, a patterned garment
Putting your hand on my forehead—yes,
It was hot—and my tongue

Was loose in my mouth, my eyes rattled
In sockets grown too large. Each part
Of myself departed from every other.
I was a grand central station of departures

A kind of wormy seedbed, like your coat
A patchwork. Baling wire was what I needed
To keep the straws of me all together.
I didn't care much. And you were gentle

You softened the pillow where my head sank
Into a swamp. You helped me settle
My parts on the raft I was floating off on.
I slept easy, knowing you were there.

You told me how to dream without dreaming
Like the roots under the snow in winter.
Dark, and knowing that darkness, warm
And held like a comfort around me.

Ann Stanford

THE IDEA OF WATER

Sitting by water
sun burning down
no shade
the idea of water
washes into your mind.
You watch the others
slowly walk
shiver a little
clasp their arms
around their chests
stand in the shallows
glittering
then scoop water
onto their upper arms
or swirl it round them
walk further
water slowly
rises up
their legs
their thighs
and they slip
into the lake.

Coolness circles their necks,
waves bobble at their lips.
Their eyes sink inside
under water
under hot sun.

But you rest
out of the shade
sitting by water
simply watching
the others
and the lake.

You feel the waves
lap into you.
The idea of water
fingers the caves
in back of your eyes
streams through
the vessel of your flesh
and coldness
deltas.
You are cooler
than the swimmers:
the water
they push back
or reach
to stroke
and hold
in their hands
slides past
but you hold it
inside yourself.
You can feel
its constant pulse
at each wrist.

   PETER STEVENS

BIRTHDAY POEM

The east wind blows a dry blanket over,
sucks the moisture from everything we touch,
especially the leaves. I crack through the loose wind
rows that roll across the path.

I waited in the closed apartment while she died,
moved in the plague of traffic and sirens.
My deep ear ached for the sound
of anything to happen.

Across the street, great trees heavy with leaves
and squirrels who travel a fine line of telephone
wire that strings things together,
taught me to measure the fall by trees,
but the dying sounds kept me from hearing
when the leaves finally touched the ground
and stacked across the path.

Today they pulled up the sheet. This is the day I was born,
but I forgot the fact that we passed each other,
she having dried to nothing that could keep her here
blew past me in her sleep, and I did not want to keep her,
seeing finally her lightness.

Anchored now with a pain that makes me sweat,
I remember my birthday three hours later,
rigid on a table, watching the ceiling,
stopping my breath to stop the hurt.
They blanket me over with a neat white sheet
to keep me warm, to keep me down,
and she sails past.

The leaves are strange strung from trees by wires,
falling, each vein, each leaf cracks to my step,

and like the snow, their sound is a pain
in the long bones of my legs.

Aware of all leaves moving, I wonder
where she will fall. I think she is the sharp
pain in my shin, but beneath everything,
leaves, dirt, sod, the worms begin to move
their sure way on, shaking the ground so slightly
I quake at the motion. The leaves' falling spins
round in my ear, and for one second I feel
the perfect pattern of her flesh passing.

JOAN STONE

THE ORDER

There was no time for questions. The order had said
"To the Woods" so they all gathered some pans, some clothes,
And piled them on top of the children in their carriages,
With sugar and meat and drink, too, carefully stowed,
For a taste of something that is good assuages,
Caressing the tongue, dread and the fear of dread.

Highways were choked with flesh. Beside the road
Sat mothers who had found they could not keep
Up with children, excited, high-spirited.
Old people sat on stones, rocking in sleep,
And here and there, on a pillow, a baby's head
Moved in a carriage that had been emptied of food.

Even a bird songless inside a cage
Had been left beside the road. Somebody cooed
For the poor little fellow, opened the narrow door,
And waited. Then, cursing ingratitude
Of a bird who stayed where it always had been before,
Threw cage and all over cliff in a towering rage.

No bird flew up from the jagged rocks below.
When shadow defined the entrance of the wood,
An unexpected coolness bathed each one
Who walked in with a strange disquietude.
Sweaters and blankets? Summer had begun
And clothes, of course, were percale and calico.

Forests have still more traps: the lashing twig,
The skulking wolf, roots arching and unlearned,
So by the morning few had not been caught.
Sugar poured from the carriages overturned
And empty, for no one had had the thought
That what seems very little can prove big,

And so the carriaged infants had all crept
From under food to find warmth under moss.
A twig can be too high to hit a child;
Hands on the ground can feel the root across,
And to the young no animal is wild.
Parents were trapped. Rocking grandparents slept

Far back along the road. A screaming horde
Of loosed, triumphant children of all ages,
Climbed trees, crawled over the limp, trapped ones
Who marred the floor of their tree-sided cage,
And no one knew which daughters or which sons
Had been the ones who first conceived the order.

NORMA McLAIN STOOP

WILL THERE BE ANY STARS IN MY CROWN

Chipping the crystal river: even at midnight
The flakes sparkle their tight arcs skyward,
One son asleep above me,
Peaking, falling, they skid and twang;
If I stop it will be the same, one body clustered,
Rampantly symmetrical, the shapes of the blessed,
The other across the room, reading.
                                     How
Do you imagine me, children? Do you see
Me crouched here, my poor knife punctual,
My sleeves full of purpose, my hands releasing
All this light?
              How patient must a man be, tending
His field, before he sees the sun feathered
In the meadowlark's breast, or
The collar of his sharp darkness?

He flies away from me.

The sun goeth down.

Ich warte.

        I can imagine one of them reading the other
To sleep, and the other dreaming the first, reading.
Thus one voice moves in two worlds, brothers, wit
Baffles the larkspur, and the moon of the dandelion
Scatters in a fit wind.
                  Are we alike
In wanting the wind to rise, lifting these chips
Beyond our grave fluency? They both sleep now
As I sleep in them, in this,

Rendering heaven.

                                    DABNEY STUART

BEYOND SILENCE II

for My Wife Fred

Once my tongue was a mirror
where angels drew their incredible songs
of sunrise and the blue haze of lilacs
sand at the road's edge sea its own psalm
but water-thieves stole from my garden
it was drought and the elms dying
dust sheeted the windows
my tongue was an old root axes had struck
struck and glanced off and blunted themselves on stone
the black weal of silence wept to itself
on that hill a plane broke into flames
a city fell like a toy before the tide
the broken legs of horses broken back of a dog
when I turned mirrors flashed and split
when I peeled my hands maggots fell to the floor
my words were cans of rotted meat
they sobbed when I tore them open
they shrivelled to a handful of tacks
they poisoned the air with a rot of teeth
nightshade and thistles were the new neighbours
only an old white goat was at ease
his one eye red with flame
his beard whispered obscenities to the wind
and where his hoofs stamped
everything died

Into this battery of burnt electrodes
this shipyard of nutshells
this tenement of broken pianos and wire
walked a flame naked as grief
in your eyes a massacre was taking place
what your fingers touched burned them with ice
when a bird sang it sang with voices of stone
flowers had the bone faces of the starved

you walked the desolate flame of sunrise and sunset
where sheep crouched by the rock wall of a pool
by the fall of a stream where it spent itself into doubt
by the stumps of burnt trees
by the tumbled bricks and the pipes still smelling of gas
by the upturned paving and the trampled coat
of someone once you'd have known
who'd hurried ahead
down alleys where only knives spoke
you licked on their lean tongues like love
in bedrooms of the dying and the dead
you were the last flicker and pallid cry of birth
till your desolate walk brought you to the pier
the peacocks of oil
the jellyfish
whips
knotting the tide

where I met you

waiting for my boat I'd made a choir of shells
they had only one song those empty tenements
and you scattered it like a child shatters night
like tide beats on a wall and breaks it down
like light opens a window on the day
in the mirror a thousand faces of us each
stored in the creases of old clothes in trunks
unfold and find the muscles of a smile

Summer
your body is a beach where boats come with their load
they heap their leaping fish into jewels for your breast
wind sings and the old men sing at dusk
staring into the sea they sing of islands of fire
islands burn in the darkness of your eyes
and the scent of wind is someone naked and close
the tide is your lover with his silver feet
my tongue is a comet in a universe of delight

a pillar of fire a Livingstone in Africa
Three Kings from the East assisting at a Birth
Siva's dance and Fuji-san and the sun

gently it pushes open a door
you are there inside but I cannot see you yet
it finds a curtain over a corridor
the walls are silk the floor and ceiling are silk
in the corridor I cannot see you yet
my tongue moves with the caution of a cat
reaches a corner pushes gently ahead
petals of the rose unfold and fold behind
smaller than a bee I fill your universe
night air is an arm holding me ah so close
it feels its way to the centre of your song
at the heart of your dance the sea murmurs and heaves
murmurs and heaves and rises to a storm
jackhammers batter the silence into stars
explode into fireflies circles of flame and flowers
water breaks into wild torrents of praise

and there you stand in the confidence of a child
and in your mouth the burning gift of a song
a new-born continent I have never sung
yourself
or is it my self
or is there only one

Andrew Taylor

DEER HERD BRINGS PUMAS TO KANSAS

a found poem

Riding in my house
Whose interior varied details such as furniture
Have been smoothed featureless by
Riding in the clouds,
The newspaper comes, claims
A few pair of puma do reside
Inside the state and growing deer
Herds probably will attract more.
Dr. Arthur Zoom of Kansas State University
Claims there are at least two pair of the big cats
In the Blue River area near the Nebraska line.
Zoom has casts of cat tracks
Identified as those of four large puma.
These casts, Zoom says, resemble clouds.

Reports have come in repeatedly
Over the past twelve years
About two of the big predator cats
Being seen northwest of Washington, Kansas,
And one pair was seen south of Manhattan
On one occasion and again last fall
Near Council Grove, Zoom said.
As they run through nearby meadows they look like clouds, Zoom said.

Wichitan Al Shot reported to Zoom
That signs of puma including tracks and distant sightings
Have been long prevalent
In the Ninnescah River area.
Shot is a bow hunter who stalks big game
In a several-state area. He has a
Colorado mountain lion (a term interchangeable with "puma")
To his bow hunting credit. When Zoom visited Shot's home,
The puma lying on the floor
Appeared to Zoom for quite a while to be a cloud.

Zoom said another pair of puma, the nation's biggest cat,
Are known to wander the Parsons-Coffeyville area,
While a pair in the Burlington vicinity
Have been seen repeatedly.
The animals probably followed along stream banks
From Colorado originally, and now that the Kansas deer herd
Is sizeable, they may multiply within the state.
Deer and smaller wild animals
Are their main fare though they have been known
To attack domestic animals.
Zoom reports that when he was visiting a farm
A few years ago, two large puma ambushed
A cow in a nearby meadow, and all three animals in the meadow
Looked like clouds tumbling across the sky.

Authenticated sighting of the puma
Is rare, Zoom explained,
Because the cat is very timid about coming near
Any point of human activity
And because it so resembles a cloud. Game officers
Have been unable to find any of the big cats
In areas where excited residents contend
The puma has visited, and there is little doubt
Some of the reports of tracks and livestock vandalism
Attributed to the puma are created by other wildlife
Including the bobcat, feral dogs, and human thieves.
Because of this, Zoom advises that hunters and farmers
Give a warning shout if they cannot make a clear
Identification. Clouds and bullets mix
But you may not want to shoot a thief, he says.

Arthur Vogelsang

SLOW COUNTRY

When you come to slow country, you will move
In the steady company
Of your hands and feet, your breath as still as a pool.
The landscape around you
Will seem as fixed as a permanent kingdom
Where the shape of the wind
Can not be found in any cloud or tree.
If your hand goes out
To a weed or a grassblade, you will have hours to spare
To wonder how it has come to be
(Before your fingers break it) that you have nothing
Of yours to reach as deeply
Between the stones. If your watch falls from your hand,
It will not break
Until it has taken time to strike the ground;
Meanwhile, you may follow it
And feel as detached as a true lord of the land
When it shatters in glassy splendor:
You will measure everything equally well thereafter.
Even spilled water
Will seem as placid and ornate as ice.
All your dear enemies,
Both real and imagined. will wait in their hiding places,
Waver, then float toward you,
More and more clearly known by sun and moonlight;
They will never reach you
Except as shrinking familiars, ripe with age.
It will seem useless
To shout in the prolonged air, since you will notice
Even a scream has a beginning,
An expansive middle, and a hapless ending
Around which the silence
Has grown more calm than ever. Between your lips
And your tongue, a sweetness;
Between your lurching heart and your wits, a passage.

Stay there. You will have time
Between the dream of embracing and the full embrace
To find your love
Lying beneath you like the willing earth,
Neither turning nor falling.

DAVID WAGONER

SNAKE HUNT

On sloping, shattered granite, the snake man
From the zoo bent over the half-shaded crannies
Where rattlesnakes take turns out of the sun,
Stared hard, nodded at me, then lunged
With his thick gloves and yanked one up like a root.

And the whole hillside sprang to death with a hissing,
Metallic, chattering rattle; they came out writhing
In his fists, uncoiling from daydreams,
Pale bellies looping out of darker diamonds
In the shredded sunlight, dropping into his sack.

As I knelt on rocks, my blood went cold as theirs.
One snake coughed up a mouse. I saw what a mouse
Knows, as well as anyone. There, beside me,
In a cleft a foot away from my braced fingers,
Still in its coils, a rattler stirred from sleep.

It moved the wedge of its head back into shadow
And stared at me, harder than I could answer,
Till the gloves came down between us. In the sack,
Like the disembodied muscles of a torso,
It and the others searched among themselves

For the lost good place. I saw them later
Behind plate glass, wearing their last skins.
They held their venom behind wide-open eyes.

DAVID WAGONER

LEST YOU, LEST POETRY

Yahweh! the tone of wind
in terrible places
and someone stumbling down
with stony phrases.

And chariots mawled in mud
one pharaohed morning
as violent as the voiced
dry bush's burning.

Keep, Lord, Your land of milk
and honey. Give hunger
lest You, lest poetry
become my stranger.

James E. Warren, Jr.

THE COUNTRY OF EVERYDAY: THE DANCER

She returns at the end of the party
to the room where the dancing was; a few guests
sprawl in the armchairs, as though stunned
by the rock still pounding from the stereo.

She returns alone. Under the exhausted stares
of the watchers, in the dim light, she begins to dance.

And reaches for the music with her body.
Beneath sweatshirt and jeans, her beautiful breasts
her lovely full hips and flanks, slowly ease her toward the sound.

Till she finds it. As the music enters her
she tries to clutch it, to hold it in against
her knees and thighs, her coaxing belly and breasts.
Her body is gripped in the beat and shudder.

She is dancing her job: working out
days making locks, the three parts
to the work of her department.
Loading in tumblers two days a week
five to a lock-blank, according to the number
stamped on a newly-cut key. Her hands
getting raw and thick from the work
dipping into the bins of tumblers
and the tray-load of fresh blanks.
Then two days inserting pins and springs
into the blanks, the company having decided
task rotation keeps down boredom to increase production.
Then two days checking the loaded locks.
But every evening, making her lunch on the kitchen table
she faces eight hours again, two cigarette breaks
and eating at noon at the same table
with the girls of her section, their chatter
of good times and boyfriends.

Before this she worked in a place that made cosmetics.

And here, on a Friday night, she dances
the dream of the girls from the plant: that they will not do this
all their lives. She dances the feverish whispers
the low, breaking voices in the bed, the marriage
that frees them from timeclock and coathook and the bus each day.
But she also knows that the new husband's face
room after room, begins to fill the entire apartment
like the smell of gas. So she dances the colour of sinks
how to vacuum a floor, and at last re-applying for her old job
as a foodstore cashier. Stepping alone in her serious beauty
she follows as well a different dream:
of a red time, pamphlets and meetings
speeches, and what is going to happen.
We won't make locks, she says. *No one will need them then.*

Now she sways to a hard music
in a room almost dark. Her nipples move
against the cloth of her shirt, sweat forms in the groin
as she flows with the sound. Her eyes are shut
as if she dances asleep
in a room of sleepers. And no one knows
the dream to awaken her.

TOM WAYMAN

THE COUNTRY OF EVERYDAY: THE GOOD CITIZEN

is water. He hears it in his house, dripping
from faucets that need new washers, feels it
inside his body: the fluids that leak
or turn sour and burn. How they flow
as they should or are blocked, and corrode.

He is aware that water enters everything. It makes paint
too runny, blotches the edge of the ceiling where it meets
the colour of the wall. Comes into sick flesh and new wood
and buckles them, makes them swell up.

Works into motors, through a crack in the distributor cap
shorting the spark, or in under the dash
to burn out the tiny bulbs of the indicator lights.
Falls heavily onto the Saturday roofs, sloping
resignedly toward the eavestroughs; runs into gutters
and ditches, and the puddles in the earthen shoulders of the roads.

It hangs in the air, luminous over a forest.
It goes away. The good citizen

knows there is not a drop in a wrist watch
that goes on ticking while you stare at it;
how a calendar, too, is perfectly dry.
You can circle a number on the pad, but the ink
dries as you wait for the day, for the hour
that is to make time flow.

Time waiting counts itself off
with a harsh sound: the dryness of paper tearing
and being crumpled, the gritty monotonous clicking
of an unoiled watchspring. The citizen

dreams like anyone else of the entirely lovely woman.
But he sees that under the bed, where his dreams end

dust clutches itself, yearning to turn
into water. And on his mattress
where he lies with the one he decides will do, love
long ago became a hair stuck on his tongue, the accidental rasp
of a toenail down skin, the moisture his fingers
usually find. And he feels
his sheets dampened with occasional pools.

The good citizen breakfasts on boiled eggs, rides
the highway to work, hours of paper and empty forms
and returns to his door and his friends' faces, evenings of
beer or music. But in all this
the good citizen uncovers a fountain.

Tom Wayman

FOOTWAY CROSSING A SUSPENSION
BRIDGE, ON THE OHIO

At the first archway past the penny toll:
A sketcher unreally sketching the skyline,
Who mammies plantation architecture down to the shore,
And nubs blacks fishing. There are two blacks fishing
By the writhe of water from the river's floor,
Close to the ani of sewers; the lettuce leaves
From warehouses bloat in the wash like corpses;
The warehouse cat sucks a fish
On the flats of foreshore mud. These
Are outside the frame of the sketcher's reference,
Which is partial; the arch of the bridge,
A levee, the manored bluffs, the fishermen.

At the second archway, the pigeons that armpit
In the iron alcoves, are all out below me
Piloting barges in the sodden water.
The buses pummeling the orange grids alongside
Set the hempensteels wingily to singing their stridencies;
The struts fret and mute. Midmost in my passage,
Here the bridge rivers me backward and upward,
Its slipstream losing my breath against the stockstill shores.
There are two shorelines, equally distant and present,
Block-housed like old prints, grayly façaded,
Me bridging the penny's worth of their difference.

At the third archway, not only I crossing:
A train in a distance, through a scrim of meshes,
Inching itself like an injured thing, crawls
To its home in the hills. The smoke it issues is substanceless;
Yet the shadow of smokes on the water is real:
Veils the light, hazes the litoral. There are two choices
At the third archway: to yearn to the farther shore
Keeping itself a handspan away,
The steepled town in its keeping equally real and unreal,

Or to return, unraveling a skein of smokes
Through labyrinthine archways to the sketcher
Who easels still in earnest the unnavigable channels
Of imagined Ohios, who easels me.
Nothing escapes the frame of the sketcher's reference
That is less than real: not the penny-romance
Of my crossing and not-crossing, not myself
Wreathed in smokes, shadows, faceless,
Painted in mid-passage, neither going nor returning.

The bridge suspends: two painted skylines, the sketcher
Who lies, me in a footway descending above inlets,
Treading grilled steps down to fished-from
And verifiable wharves. I have told
My secrets to the Ohio: there are no islands.

       NANCY G. WESTERFIELD

LET IT BLOW

Let it blow, said the union of amalgamated winds,
And let it drip, said the cloud trust.
Where is there an end to it,
The self-interest?
—Whither my feet takest me I find lobbying,
Invented by Joseph Lobby,
Who wrote a nonpartisan editorial in behalf of his own candidacy
    for alderman in a tiny New England slum housing development
    in 1802.

Now each purple mountain majesty requires a private sunrise.
We pass individually unto grace, cutting each other on the thruway,
Singing the brotherhood of one.

Let it blow;
Let the assorted selves drop leaflets against litter,
Picket the morning.

Who will volunteer to park in a bus stop?
Foul the word supply?

—The right of the people to keep and bear arms shall not be infringed
Nor other rights of the righteous
So that the pharmaceutical firms may suck forever
On the inner heart of our headache.

How can a nation of smart cookies be so dumb?
Did Jefferson do it? Hamilton? Thoreau maybe?

—I look into the kindly eyes of my anarchist soul mate,
She (he) dreaming of a Greek isle with her (his) American Express card,
She (he) wanting 400 hp and a water bed
    (and a mountain, a guru, and an independent income).

Not an institution in this country is not betrayed by its souls
    in residence.

Who is left to pull the weeds from the Xerox machine?
Where will we find the manpower to carry this week's privateering to
 the town dump?

--Let it blow,
And let the associations for the preservation of freedom publish the
 unexpurgated results
At a profit.

REED WHITTEMORE

A STORM IN APRIL

Some winters, taking leave,
Deal us a last, hard blow,
Salting the ground like Carthage
Before they will go.

But the bright, milling snow
Which throngs the air today—
It is a way of leaving
So as to stay.

The light flakes do not weigh
The willows down, but sift
Through the white catkins, loose
As petal-drift,

Or in an up-draft lift
And glitter at a height,
Dazzling as summer's leaf-stir
Chinked with light.

This storm, if I am right,
Will not be wholly over
Till green fields, here and there,
Turn white with clover,

And through chill air the puffs of milkweed hover.

RICHARD WILBUR

JOHN CHAPMAN

Beside the Brokenstraw or Licking Creek,
Wherever on the virginal frontier
New men with rutting wagons came to seek
Fresh paradises for the axe to clear,

John Chapman fostered in a girdled glade
Or river-flat new apples for their need,
Till half the farmsteads of the west displayed
White blossom sprung of his authentic seed.

Trusting in God, mistrusting artifice,
He would not graft or bud the stock he sold.
And what, through nature's mercy, came of this?
No sanguine crops of vegetable gold

As in Phaeacia or Hesperides,
Nor those amended fruit of harsher climes
That bowed the McIntosh or Rambo trees,
Ben Davis, Chandler, Jonathan, or Grimes,

But the old *Malus malus,* doubled-dyed,
Eurasia's wilding since the bitter fall,
Sparse upon branches as perplexed as pride,
An apple gnarled, acidulous, and small.

Out of your grave, John Chapman, in Fort Wayne,
May you arise, and flower, and come true.
We meanwhile, being of a spotted strain
And born into a wilder land than you,

Expecting less of natural tree or man
And dubious of working out the brute,
Affix such fruitful scions as we can
To the rude, forked, and ever savage root.

RICHARD WILBUR

AFTER THE CREATION

1

Beetle dozing in the moist clay,
Your bright shell
Pumping like a heart;

I watched you crawling
In the striped darkness of the shed;
You resembled an eyelid drooped in the dirt,
A wilted prayer,
Smelling of pepper and dead books.

Rust-colored seed clenched in brightness.

2

From you I inherit my patience
With pure horror;
My faceted eyes, all but one of their gleams
Turned inward;
My dread of footsteps;
My self-knowledge.
It's that simple.

3

Because your scrapes and clicks
Are brothers
To all the small tongues of earth.
Because you outnumber me
In my solitude.
Because, like God, you are everywhere.
Because the world is manna to beetles.

4

I dreamt my heart was a beetle
With paralyzed bolts for legs.

It brushed my skin
With its bare wires, and I had
The revelation of stone.
It twitched in the passageways
Of my throat, and I knew
The cold fire of need.
It ate me from within, creating hunger
And the seasons of flesh.
It died, and left me with a book of skin,
My only honesty.

5

But when the beetle unfolds its stubby wings,
When its eyes wander like watery pins,
There will be nothing.

No childhood killed over again
Before your eyes.
Nothing to creep wildly in the insomniac streets.
Nothing adrift in the ominous peacefulness
Of work and love.

God's chitinous claw descends
Like a snowflake,
And the beetle of the first day,
The life-lode,
Starts over again its countdown toward nightmare.

PAUL ZWEIG

DATE DUE

PR
1225
.B65
v. 26

Best poems.

DATE DUE			
FEB 14 1978			
DEC 18 1984			

351064

MAAG LIBRARY
YOUNGSTOWN STATE UNIVERSITY
YOUNGSTOWN, OHIO

APR 26 1976